ALPHABET A-Z

TRACING AND COLORING WORKBOOK

INCLUDES WORD GAMES, WORD FINDS AND MORE!
INCLUDES AN ANSWER KEY.

STEP 1 : LEARNING THE ALPHABET AND COLORING
STEP 2 : TRACING LETTERS
STEP 3 : WRITING SIGHT WORDS

This Handwriting workbook helps kids of all ages to start learning letters of the alphabet and to improve their handwriting and coloring.

Name:

Class:

ALPHABET A-Z

The alphabet is the set of 26 letters
(from A to Z)

A B C D E
F G H I J
K L M N O
P Q R S T
U V W X Y
Z

Name: _______________   Class: _______________

Aa

alligator

Bb

bee

Cc

cat

Dd

deer

Ee

elephant

Ff

frog

Gg

giraffe

Hh

horse

iguana

jellyfish

koala

lion

Mm

monkey

Nn

newt

Oo

octopus

Pp

pig

Qq

quail

Rr

rabbit

Ss

sheep

Tt

tiger

Uu

unicorn

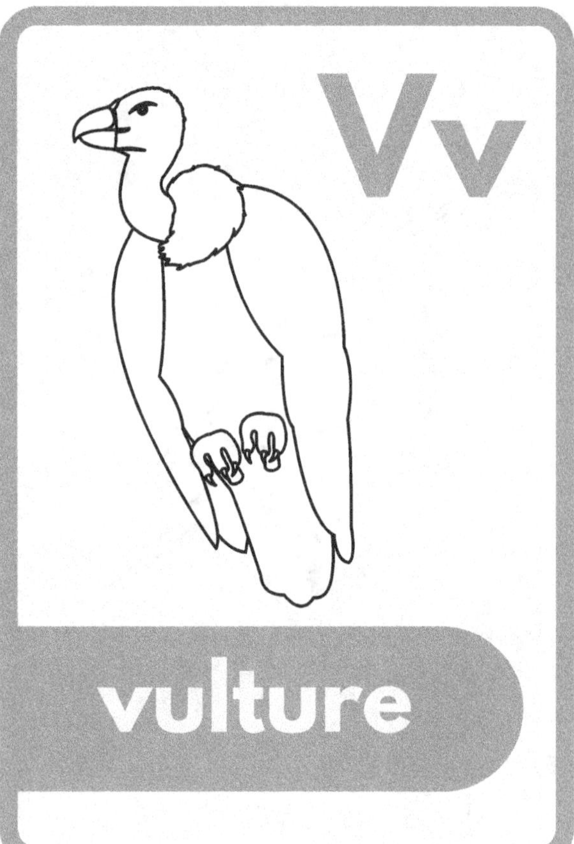

Vv

vulture

Ww

walrus

Xx

xenops

Yy
yak

Zz
zebra

A
B C

TRACING LETTERS

Practice writing the alphabet by tracing the letters below.

Aa Bb Cc Dd

Ee Ff Gg Hh

Ii Jj Kk Ll

Mm Nn Oo Pp

Qq Rr Ss Tt

Uu Vv Ww Xx

Yy Zz

All about the Letter A

Trace the Letter A

Aa Aa Aa Aa

Aa Aa Aa Aa

Aa Aa Aa Aa

All about the Letter B

Trace the Letter B

Bb   Bb   Bb   Bb

Bb   Bb   Bb   Bb

Bb   Bb   Bb   Bb

All about the Letter C

Trace the Letter C

Cc Cc Cc Cc

Cc Cc Cc Cc

Cc Cc Cc Cc

All about the Letter D

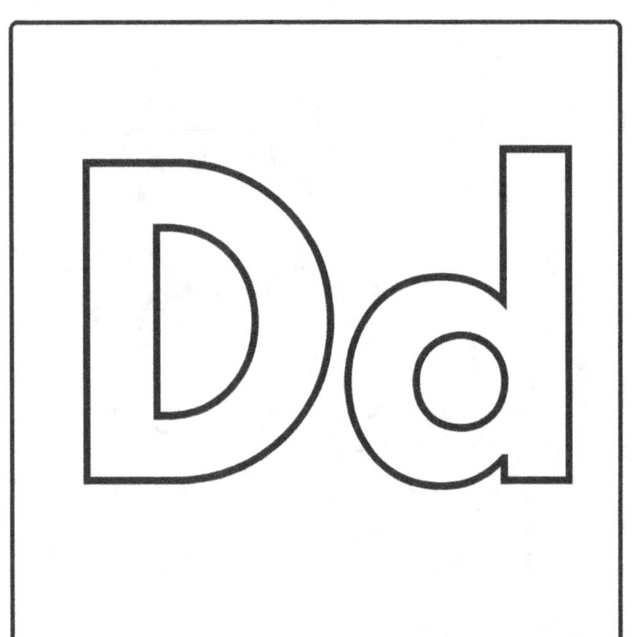

Trace the Letter D

Dd Dd Dd Dd

Dd Dd Dd Dd

Dd Dd Dd Dd

All about the Letter E

Trace the Letter E

Ee Ee Ee Ee Ee
Ee Ee Ee Ee Ee
Ee Ee Ee Ee Ee

All about the Letter F

Trace the Letter F

All about the Letter G

Trace the Letter G

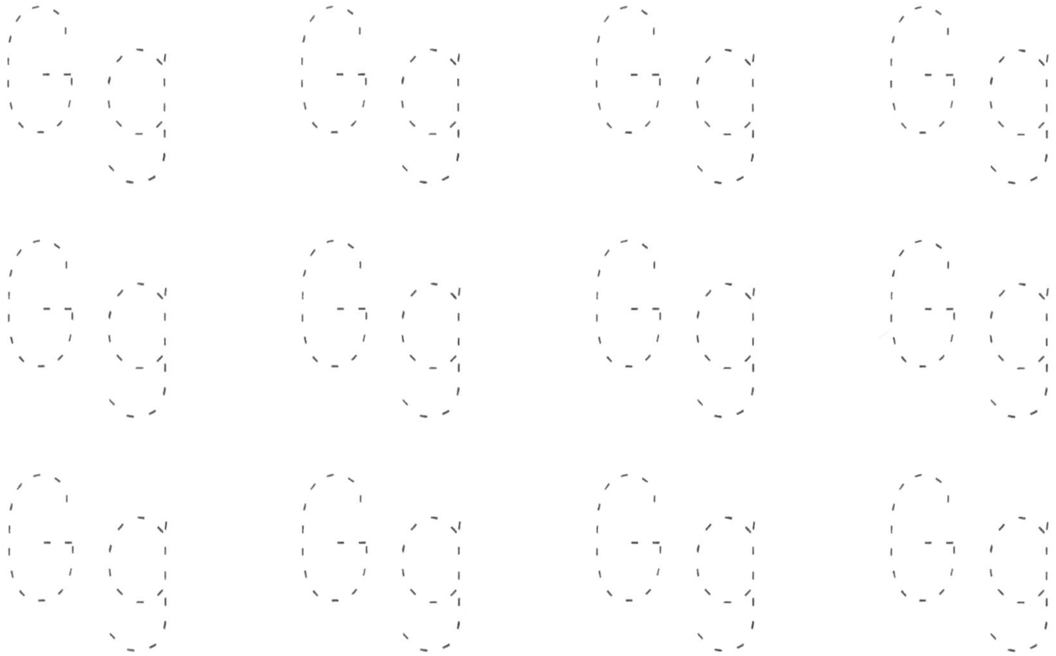

All about the Letter H

Trace the Letter H

Hh Hh Hh Hh

Hh Hh Hh Hh

Hh Hh Hh Hh

All about the Letter I

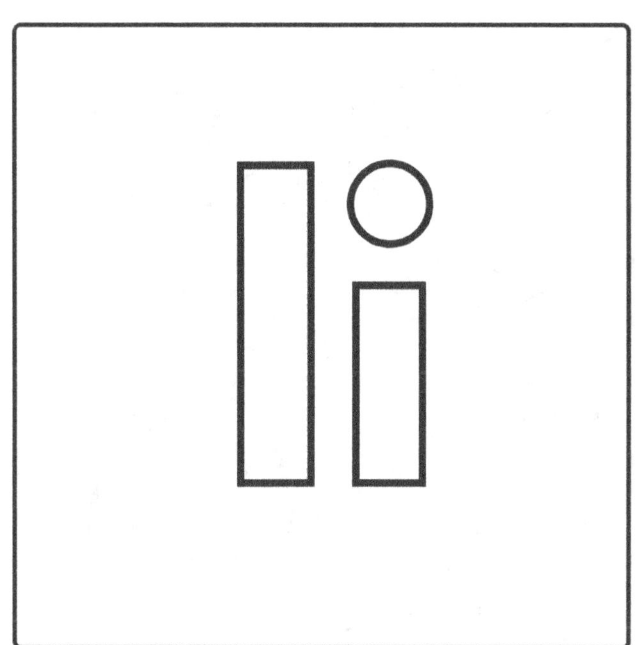

Trace the Letter I

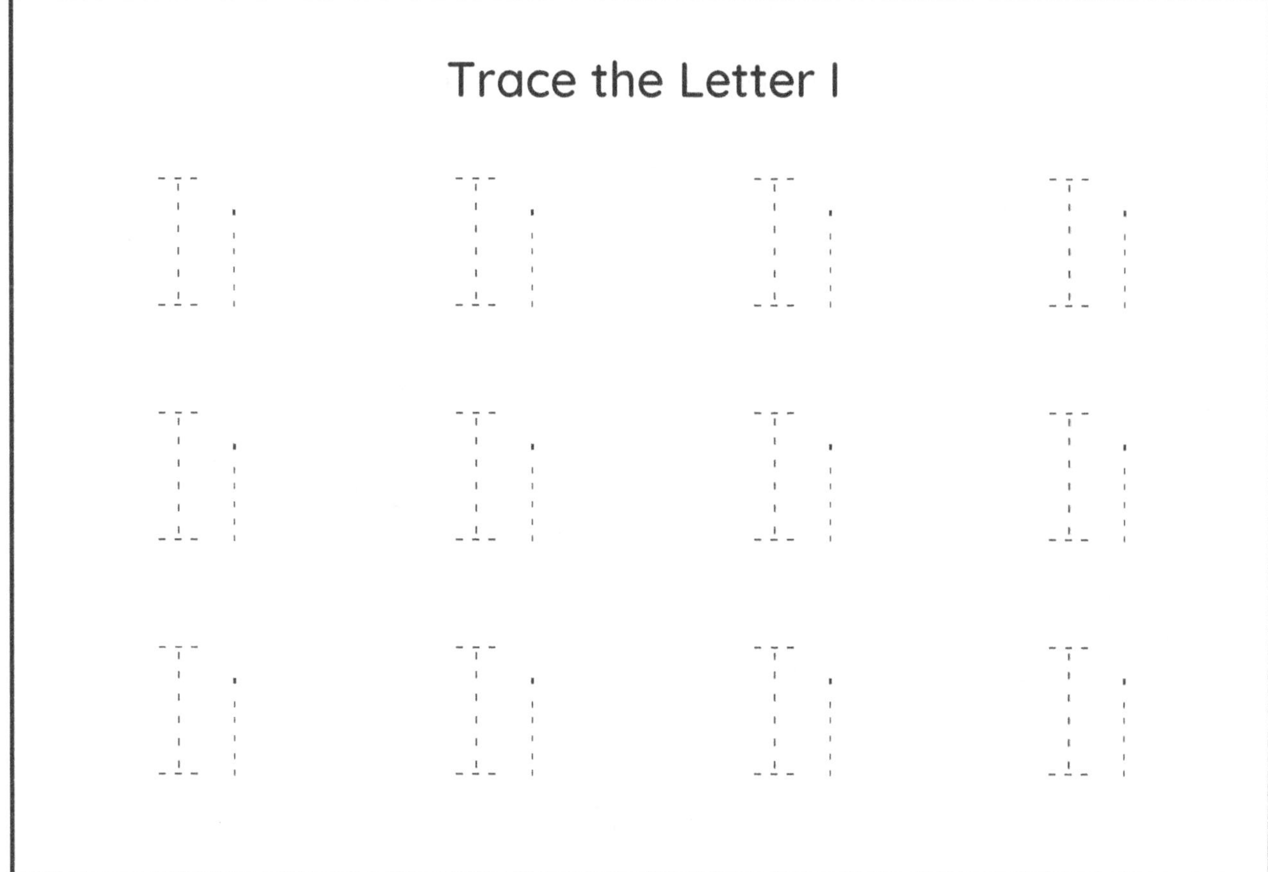

All about the Letter J

Trace the Letter J

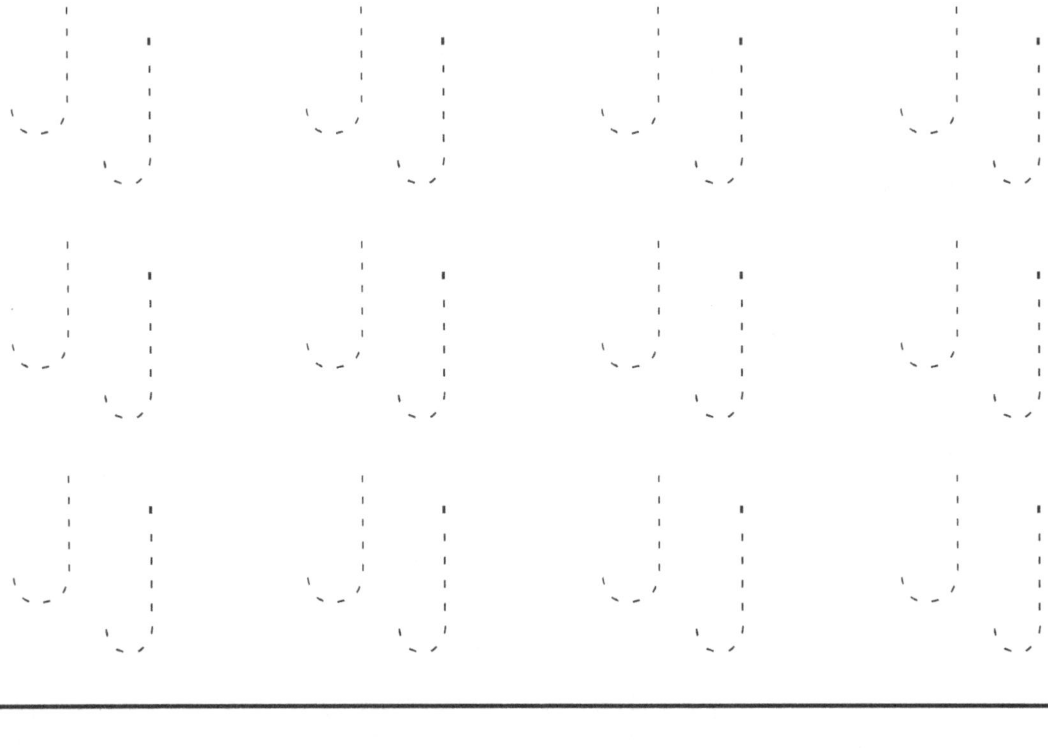

All about the Letter K

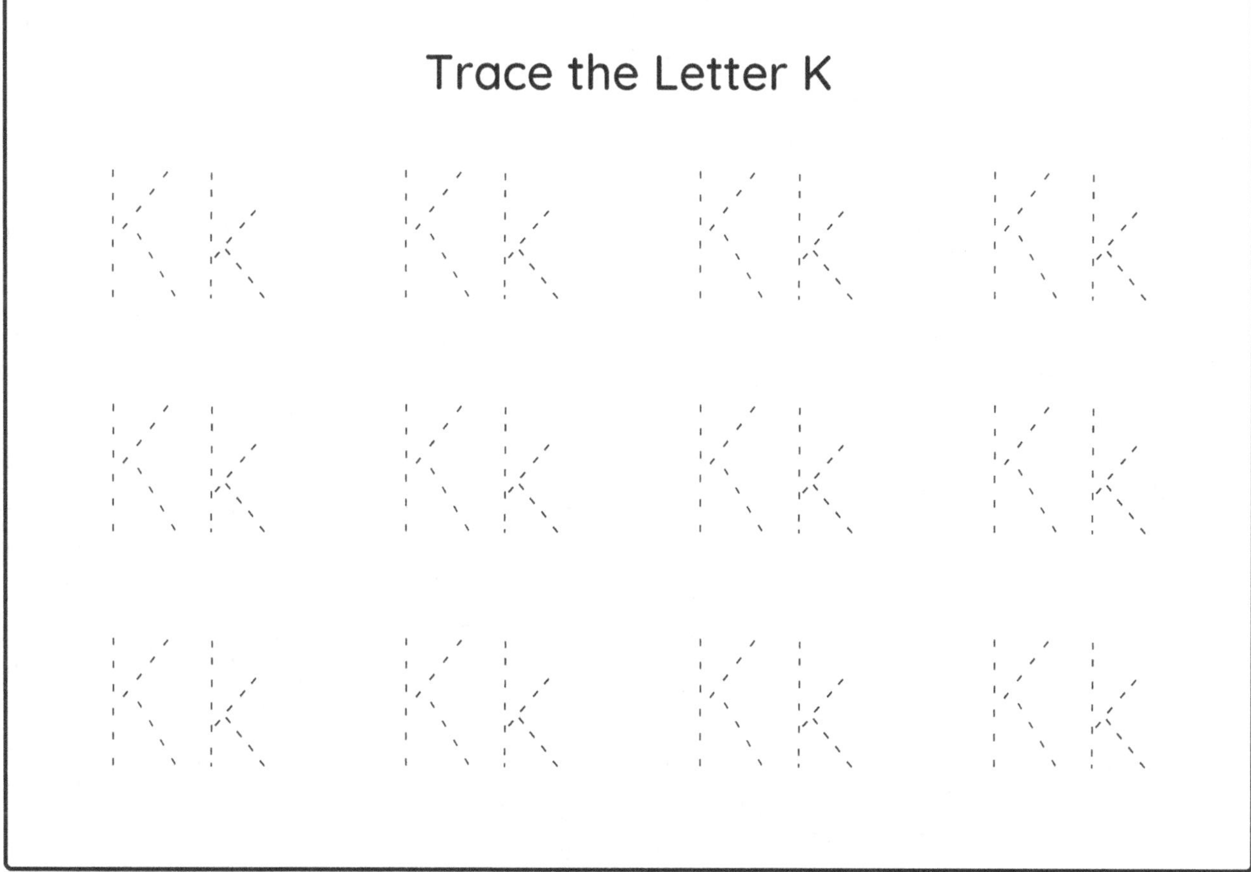

Trace the Letter K

All about the Letter L

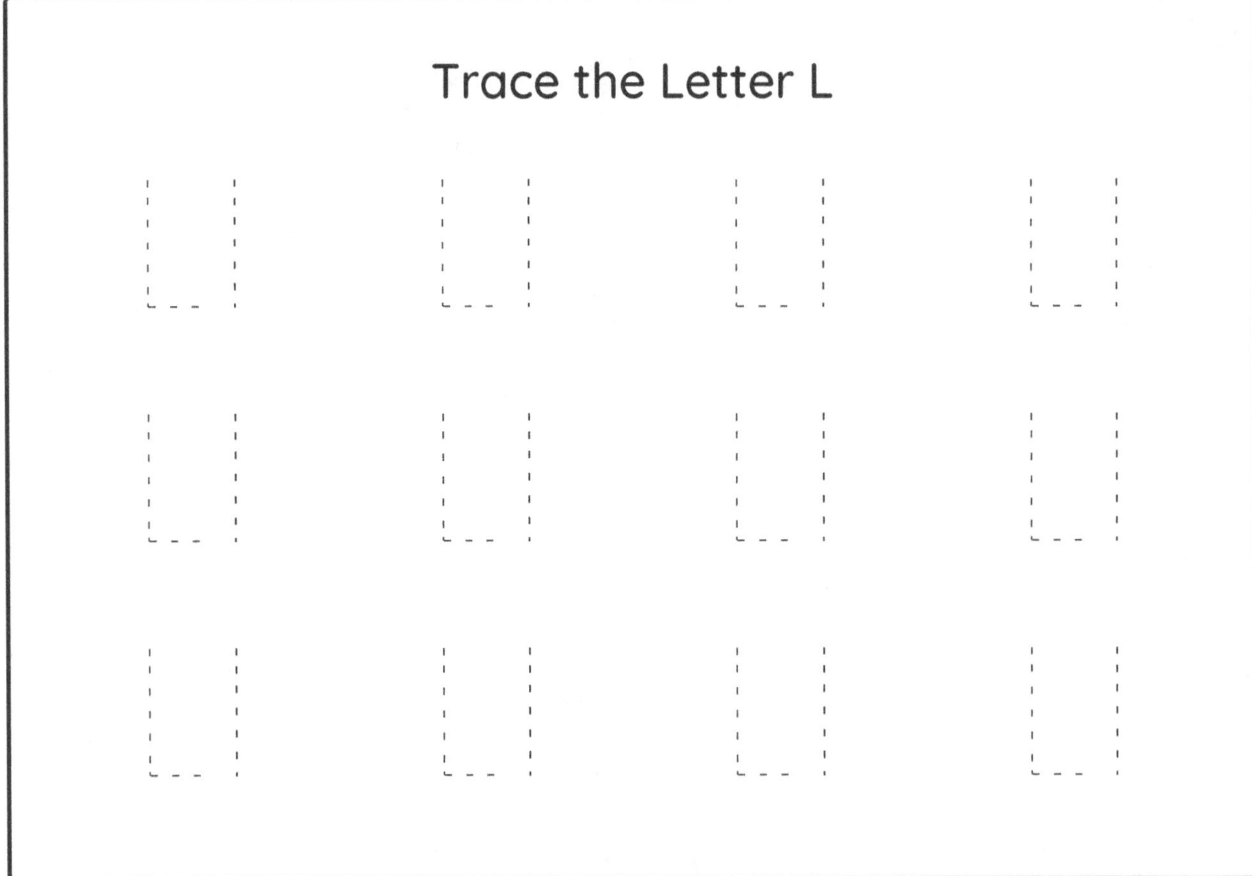

Trace the Letter L

All about the Letter M

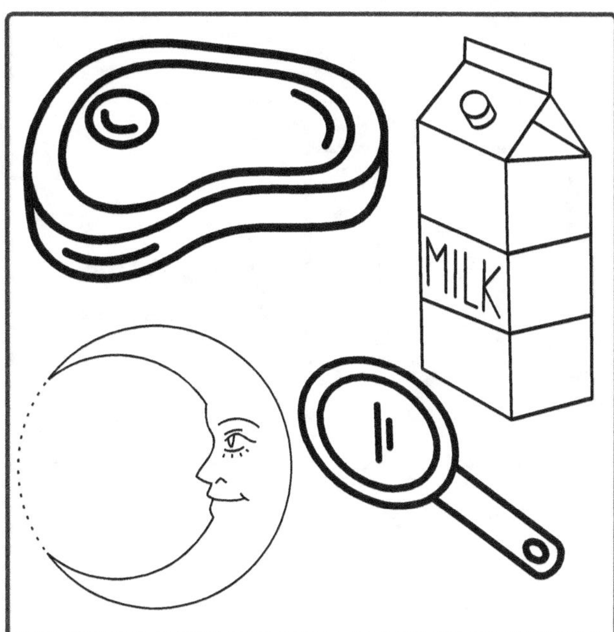

Trace the Letter M

Mm Mm Mm Mm

Mm Mm Mm Mm

Mm Mm Mm Mm

All about the Letter N

Nn

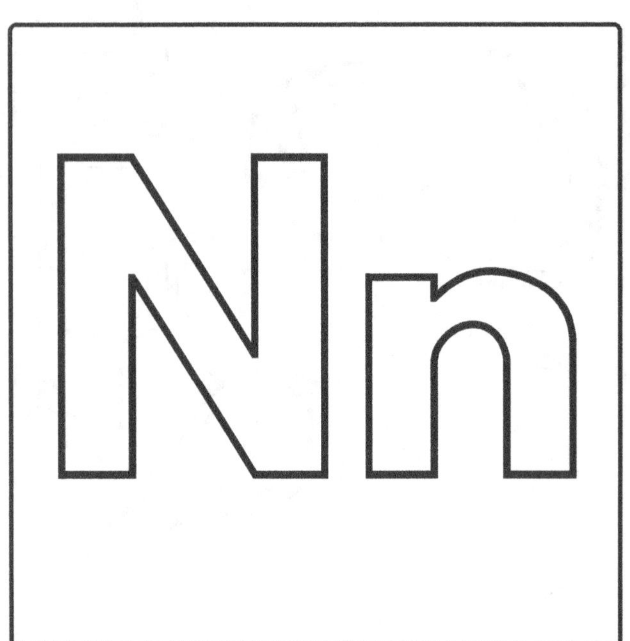

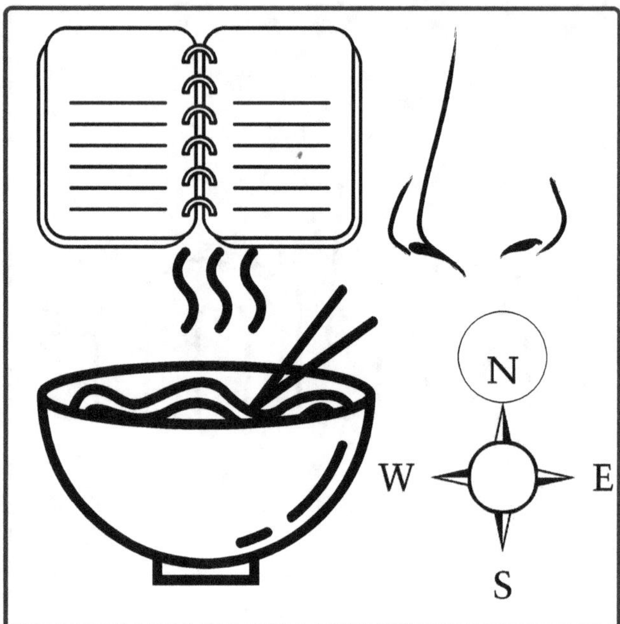

Trace the Letter N

Nn Nn Nn Nn

Nn Nn Nn Nn

Nn Nn Nn Nn

All about the Letter O

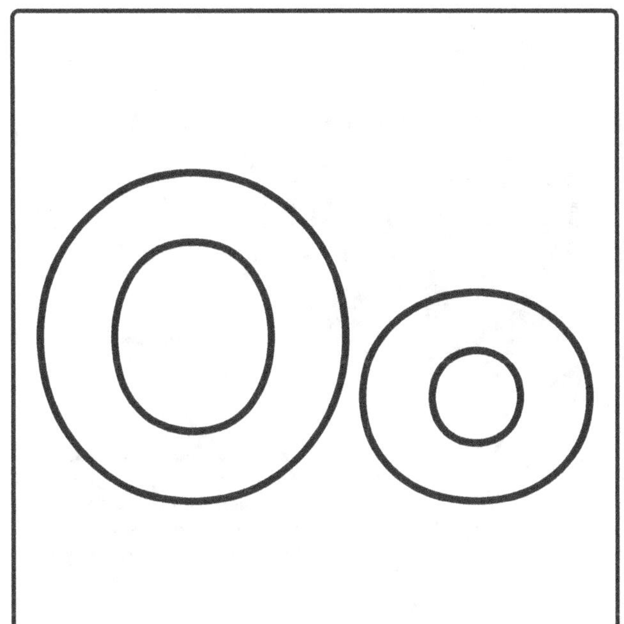

Trace the Letter O

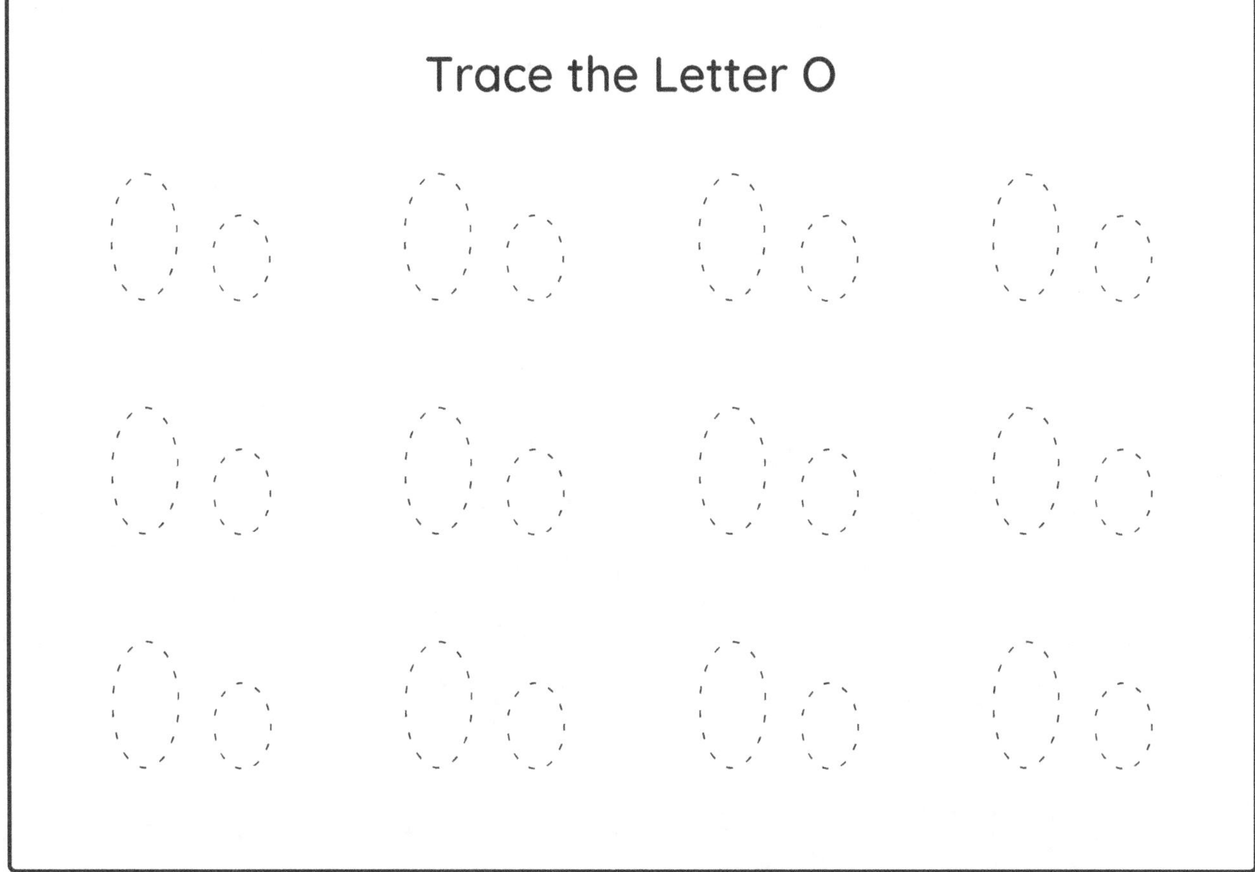

All about the Letter P

Pp

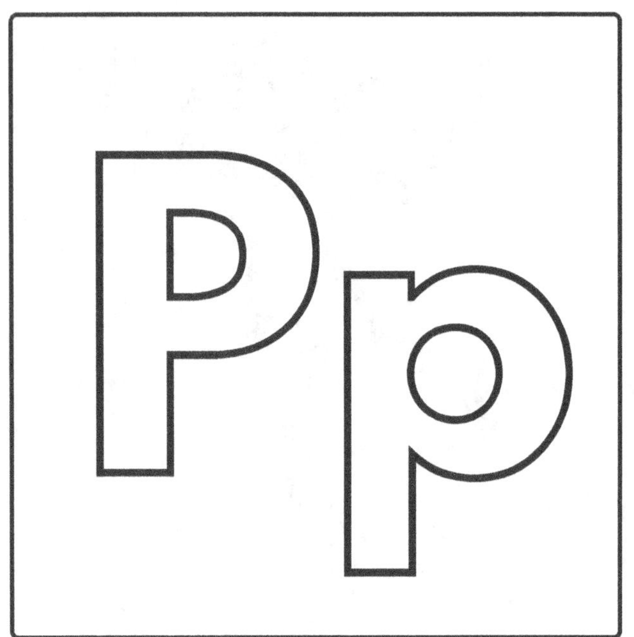

Trace the Letter P

Pp Pp Pp Pp

Pp Pp Pp Pp

Pp Pp Pp Pp

All about the Letter Q

Trace the Letter Q

Qq Qq Qq Qq
Qq Qq Qq Qq
Qq Qq Qq Qq

All about the Letter R

Trace the Letter R

Rr Rr Rr Rr

Rr Rr Rr Rr

Rr Rr Rr Rr

All about the Letter S

Trace the Letter S

All about the Letter T

Trace the Letter T

All about the Letter U

Trace the Letter U

Uu Uu Uu Uu

Uu Uu Uu Uu

Uu Uu Uu Uu

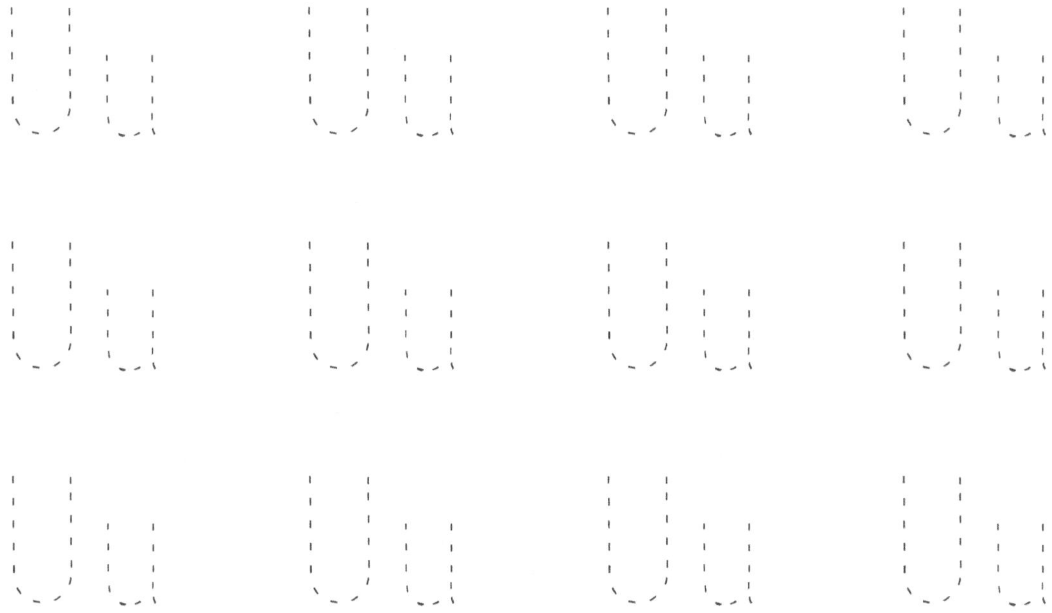

All about the Letter V

Vv

Trace the Letter V

V v V v V v V v

V v V v V v V v

V v V v V v V v

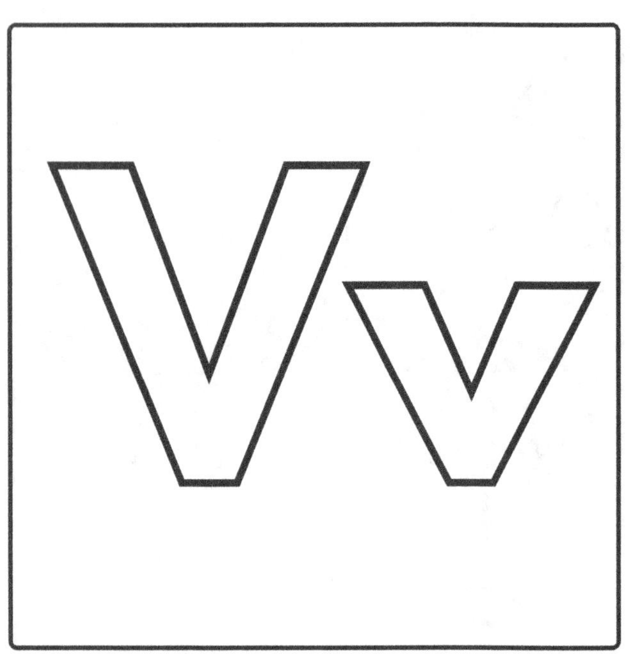

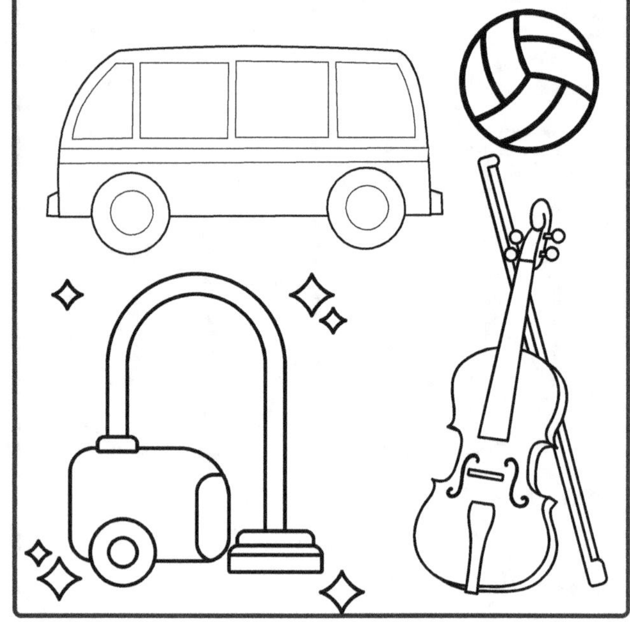

All about the Letter W

Ww

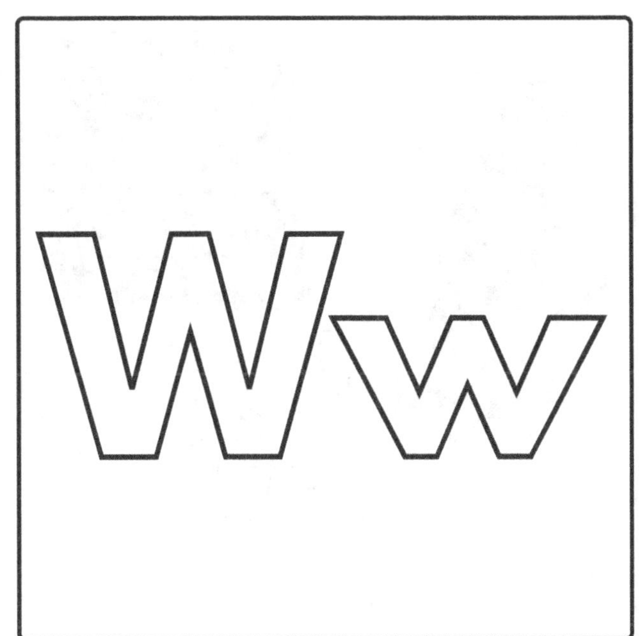

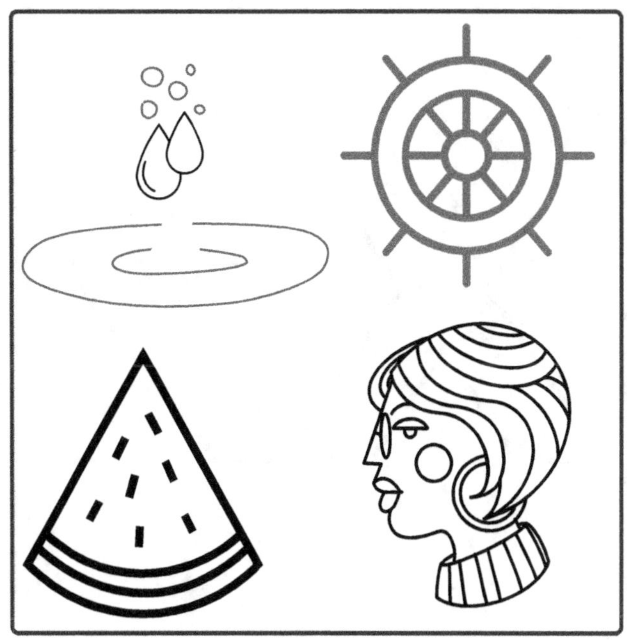

Trace the Letter W

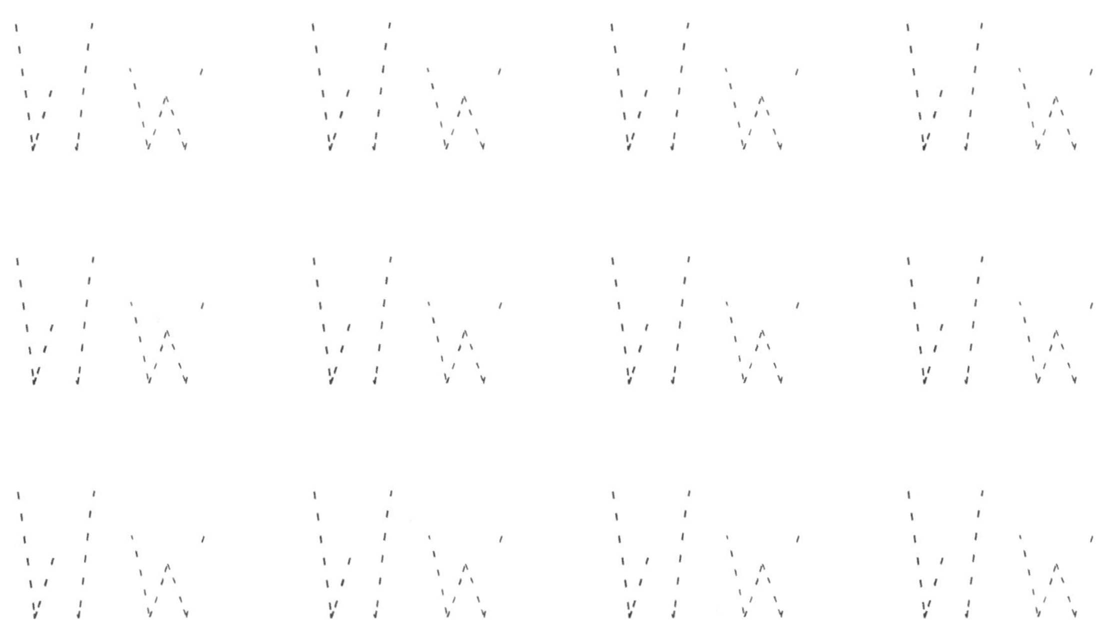

All about the Letter X

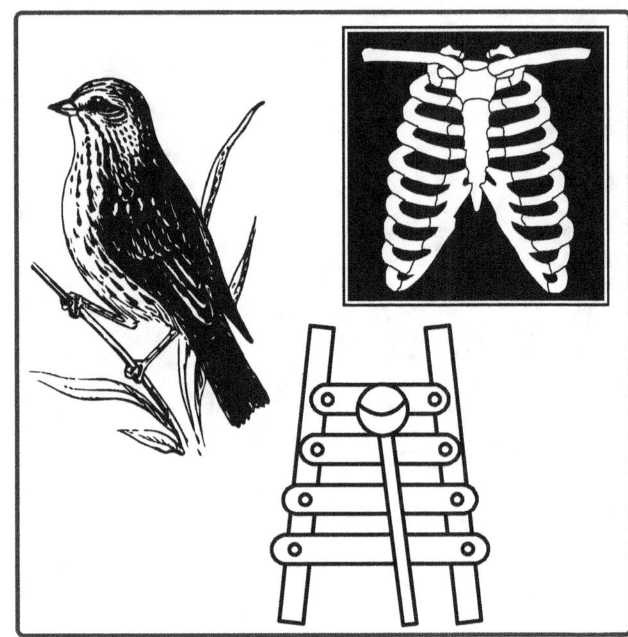

Trace the Letter X

All about the Letter Y

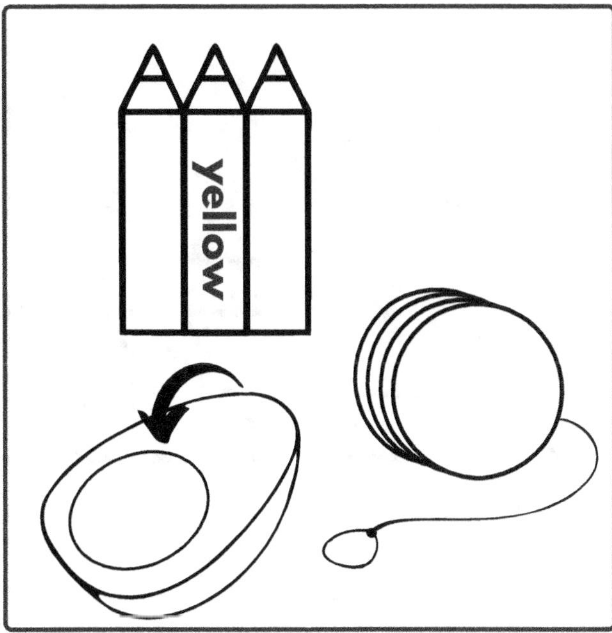

Trace the Letter Y

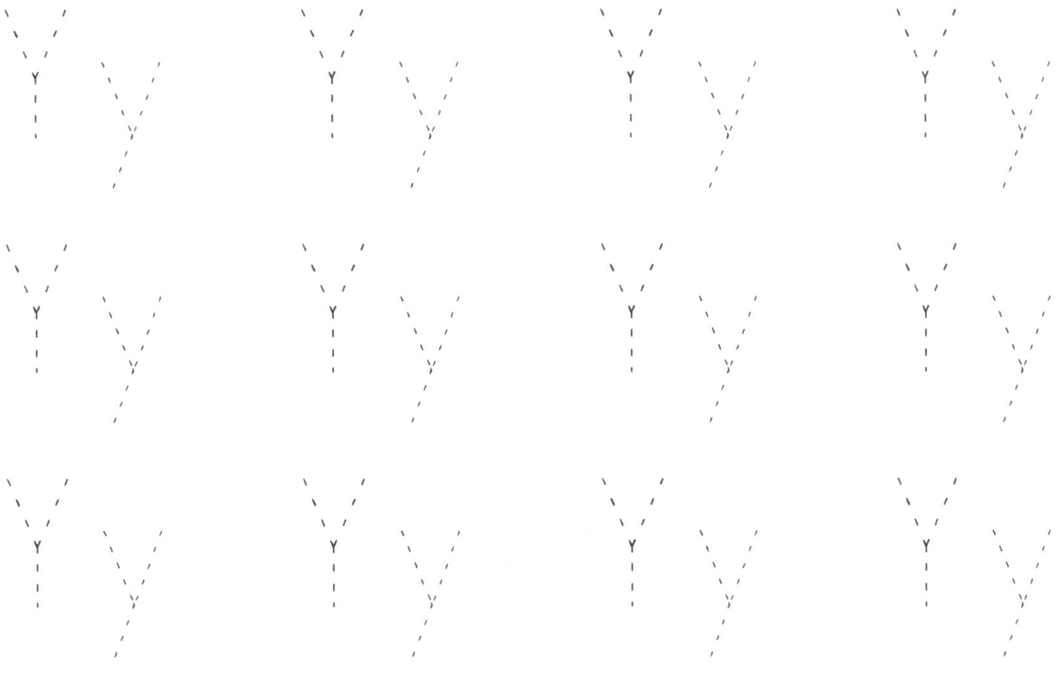

All about the Letter Z

Trace the Letter Z

Spot the Letters

Look at the letter on the left and circle the
same letters on the row.

b	b	o	c	d	b	e
k	d	m	k	l	k	k
e	j	e	v	m	e	k
c	c	a	c	d	c	e
o	o	m	n	o	f	l
q	g	h	i	k	p	q
z	x	w	z	z	s	q

Spot the Letters

Look at the letter on the left and circle the
same letters on the row.

d	b o c d b e
p	d m k l p p
j	j w v m e j
t	w a t d c t
n	i m n o n l
g	g h i g p q
i	j w m l k i

Letter Hunt

Find and color the letter A

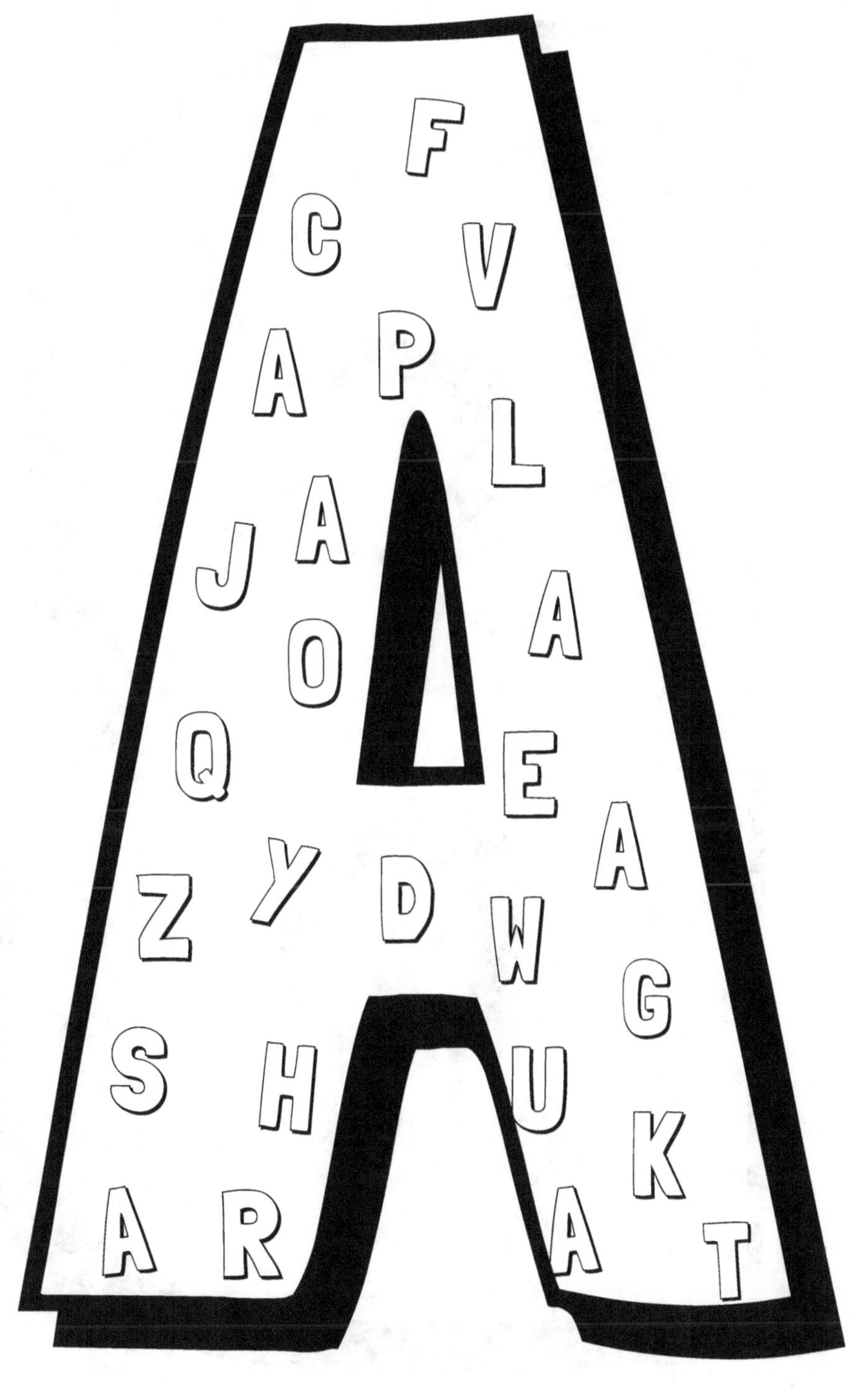

Letter Hunt

Find and color the letter B

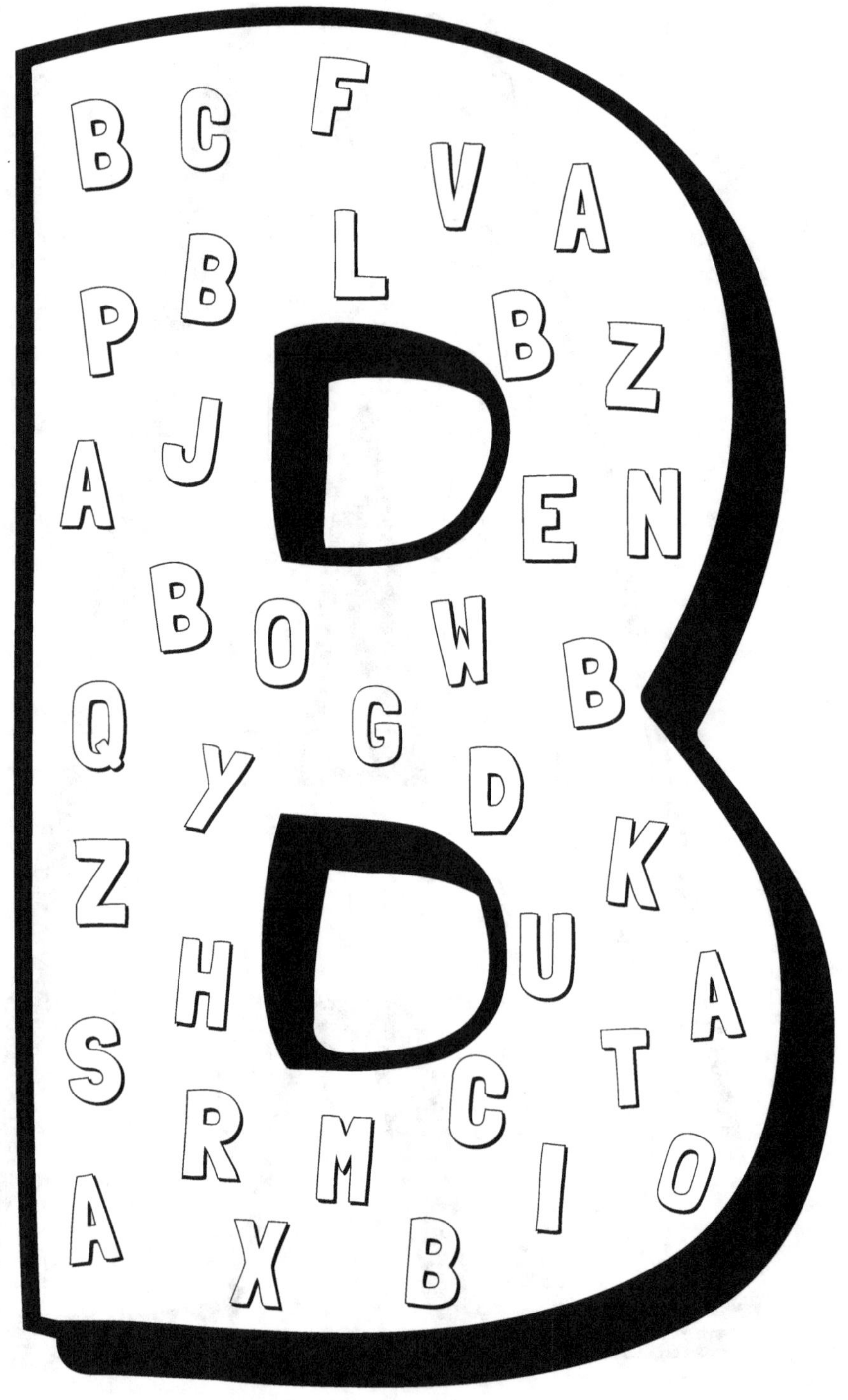

Letter Hunt

Find and color the letter C

Letter Hunt

Find and color the letter D

Letter Hunt
Find and color the letter E

Letter Hunt

Find and color the letter F

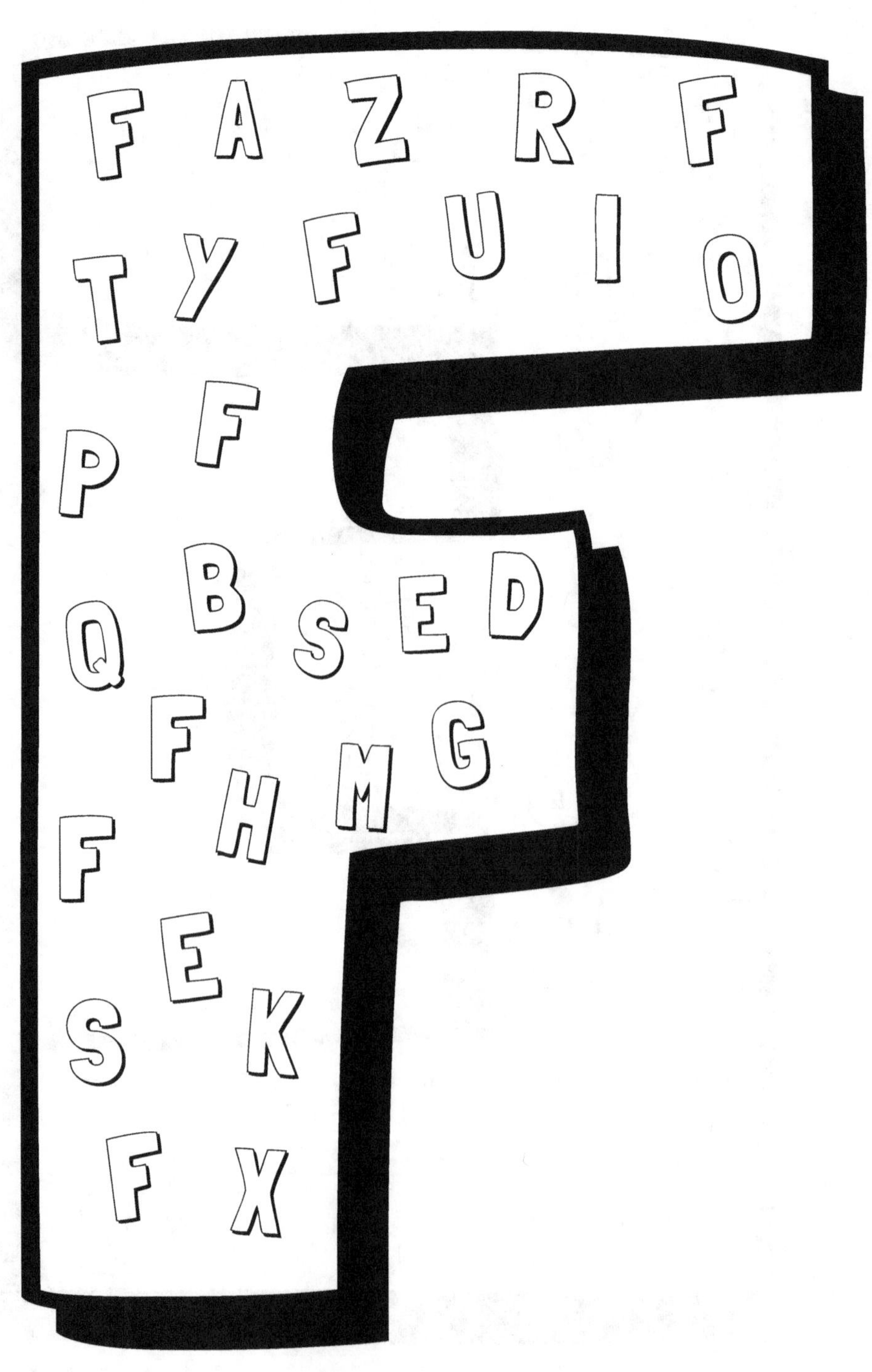

Letter Hunt

Find and color the letter G

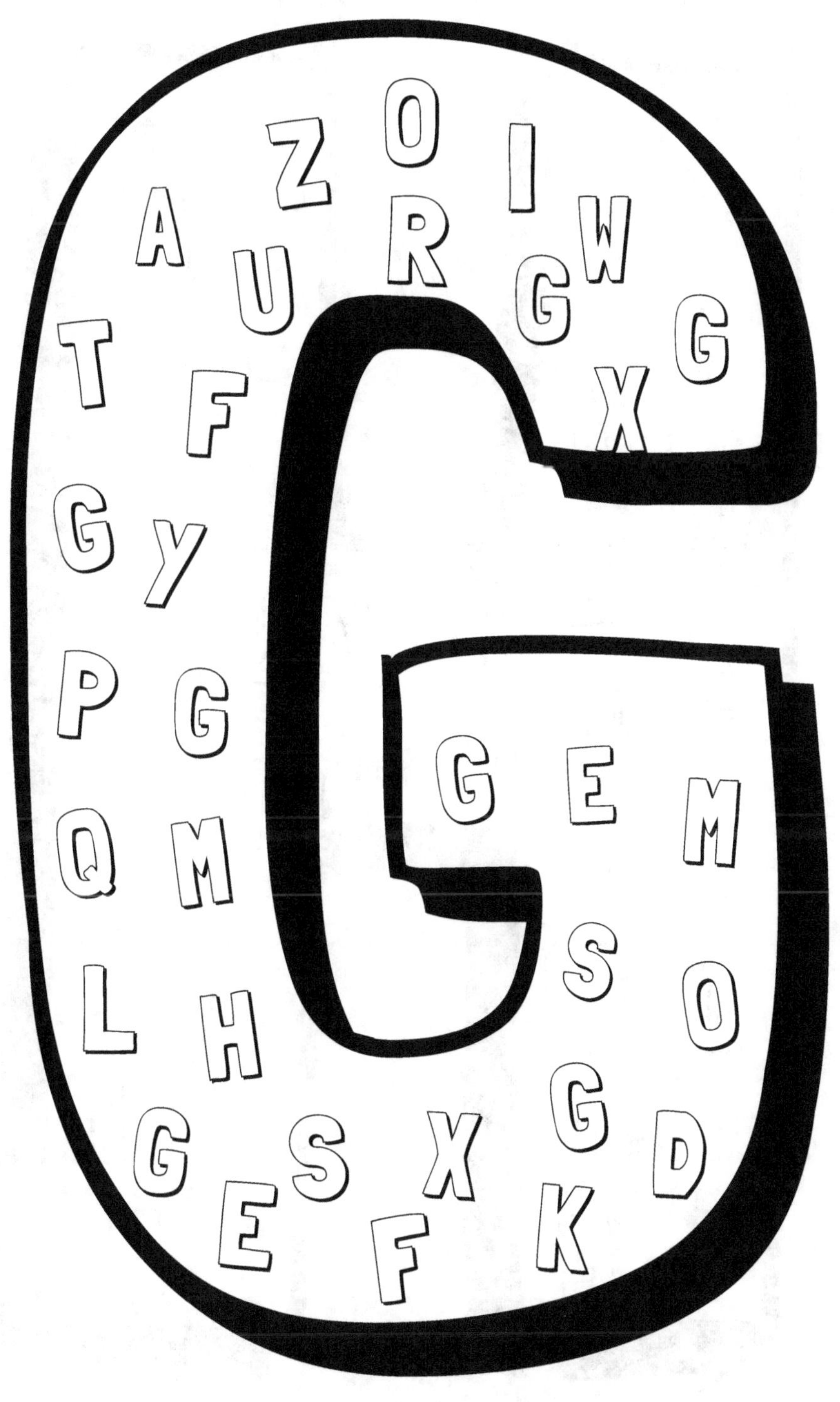

Letter Hunt

Find and color the letter H

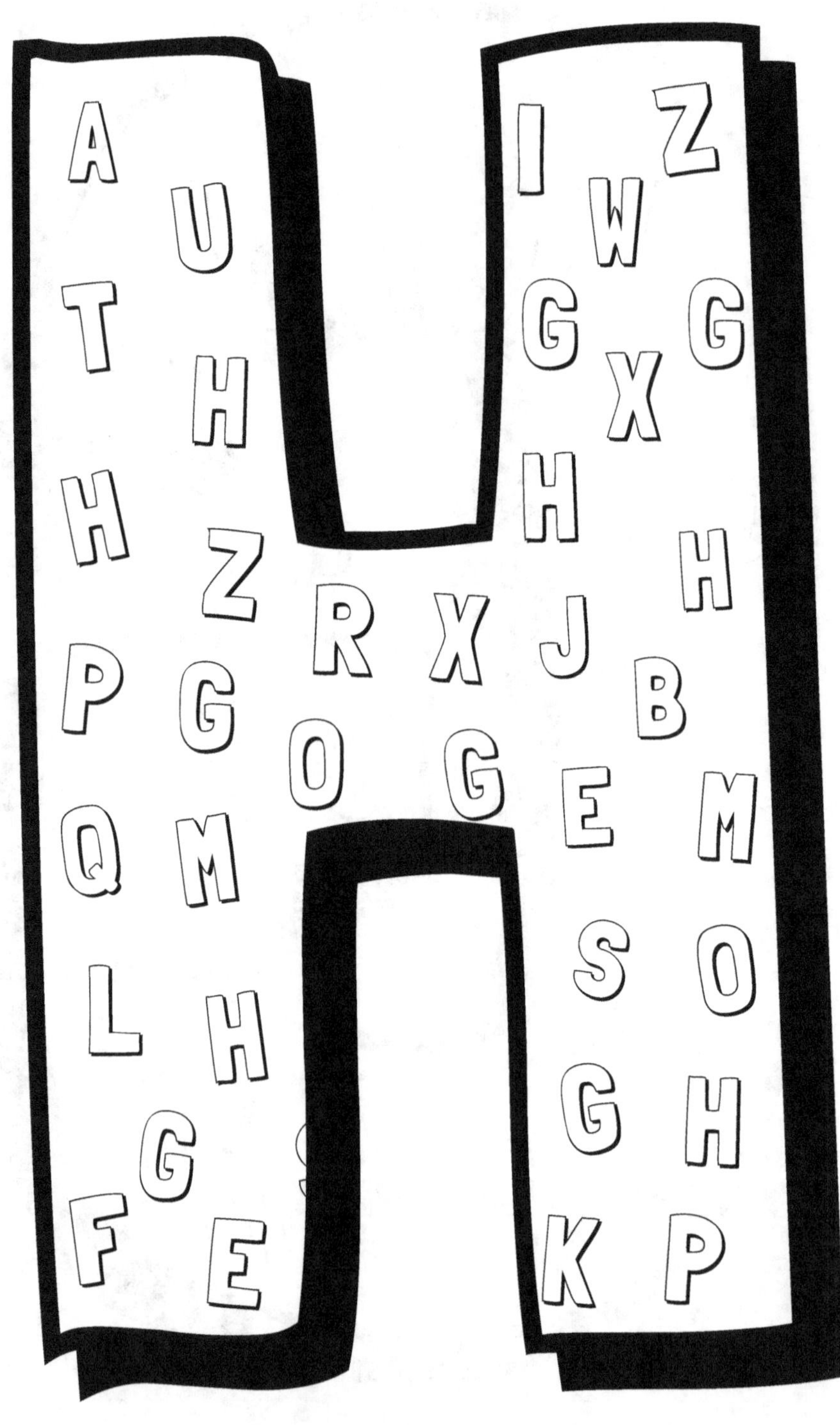

Letter Hunt

Find and color the letter I

Letter Hunt

Find and color the letter J

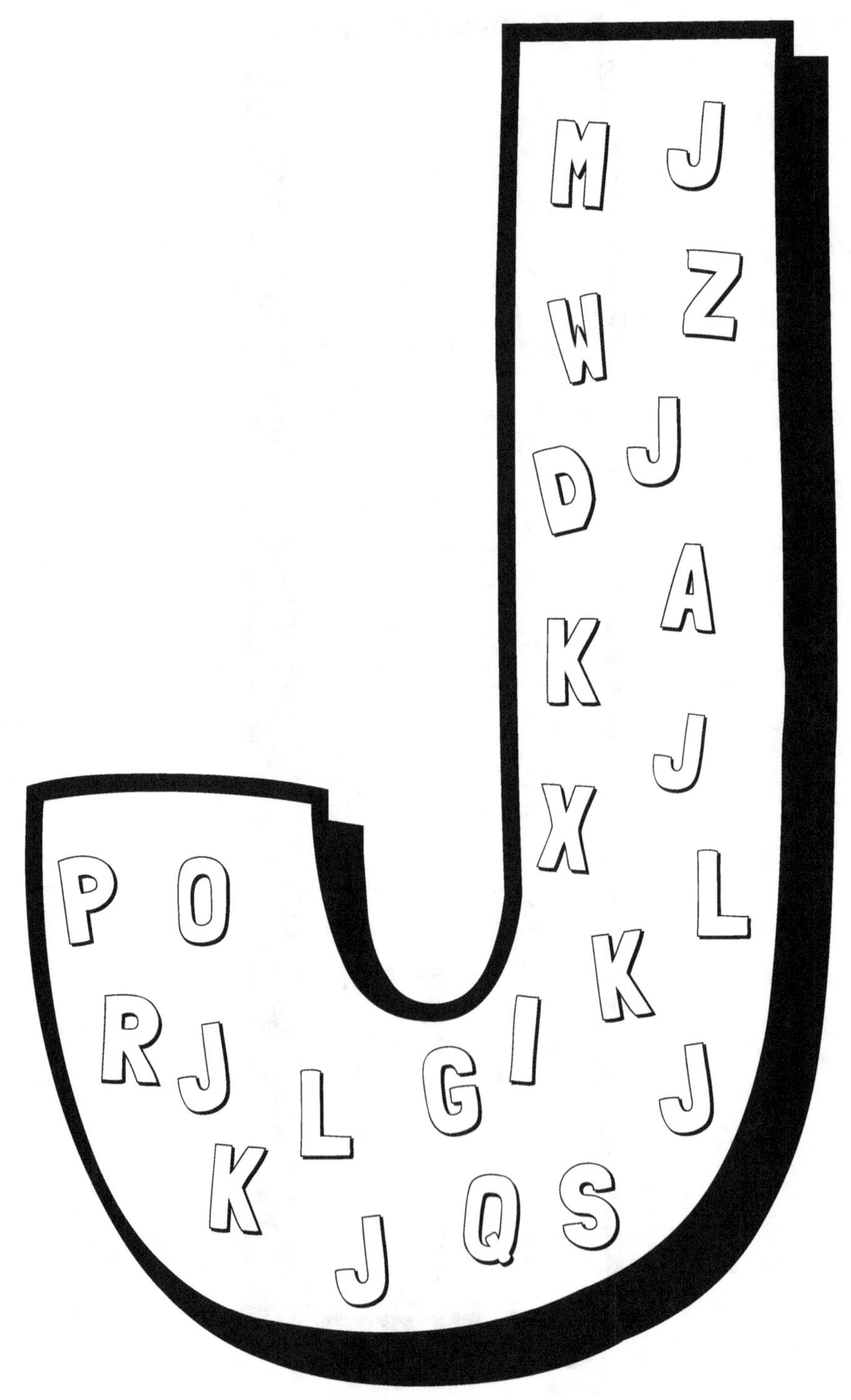

Letter Hunt

Find and color the letter K

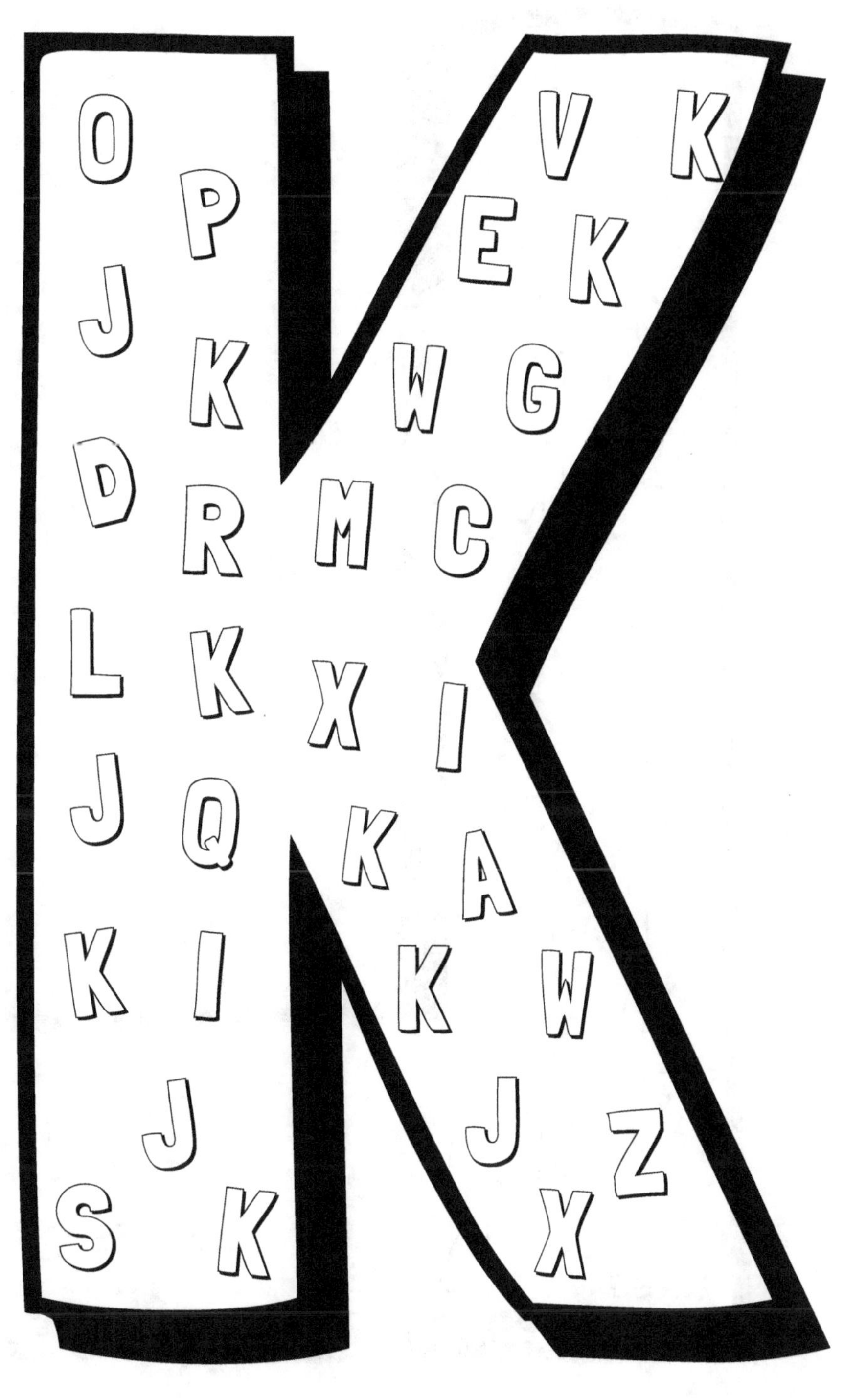

Letter Hunt

Find and color the letter L

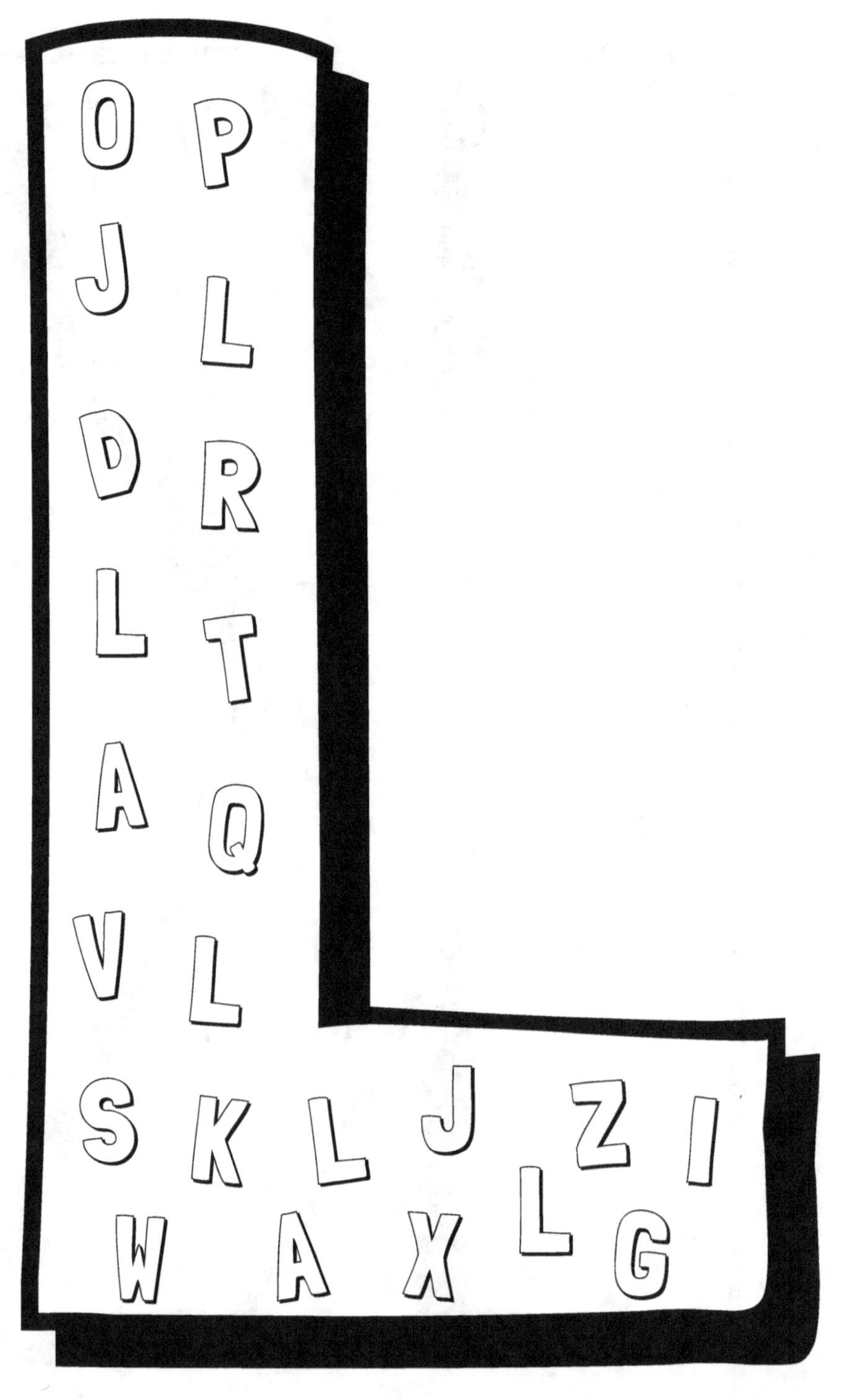

Letter Hunt

Find and color the letter M

Letter Hunt

Find and color the letter N

Letter Hunt

Find and color the letter O

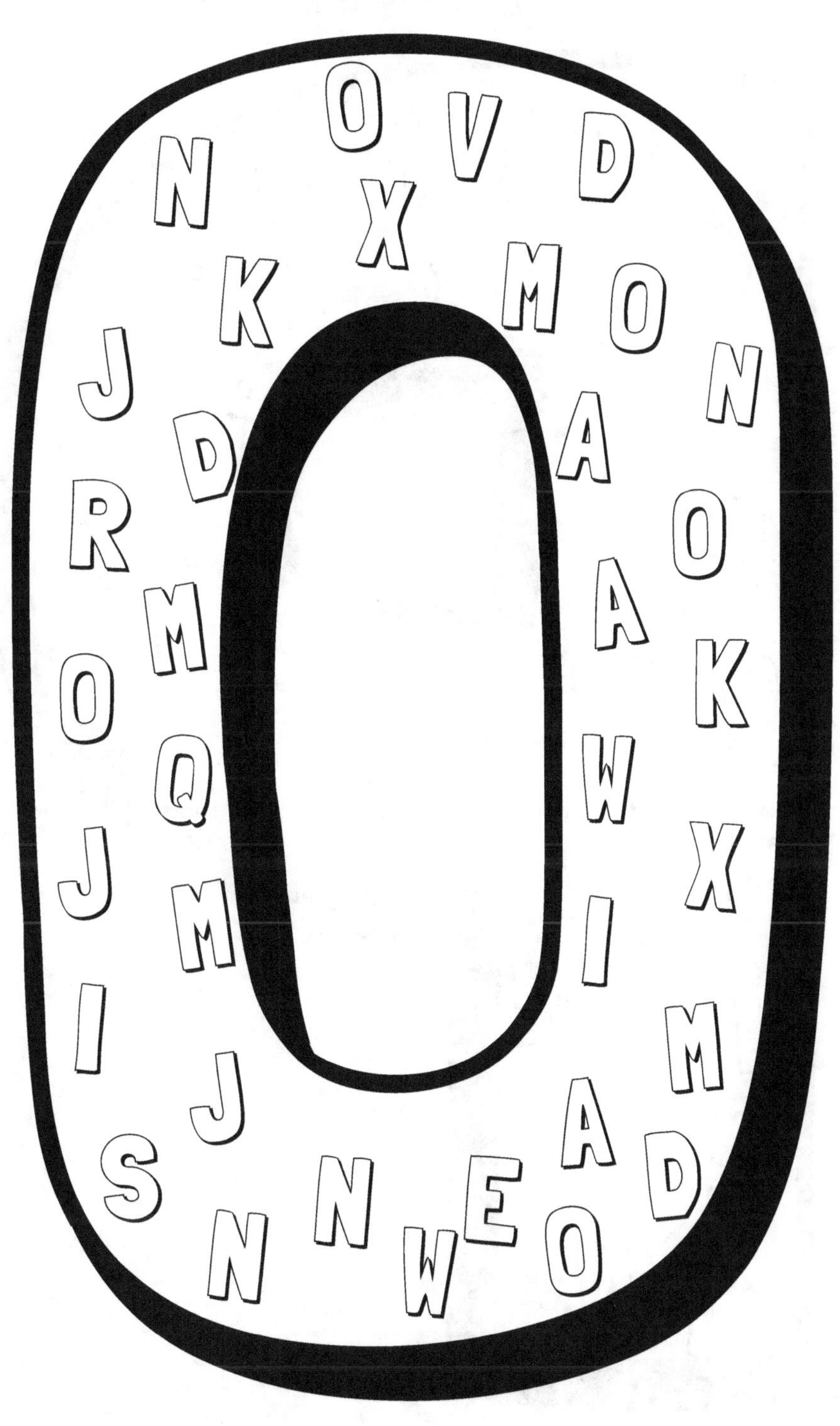

Letter Hunt

Find and color the letter P

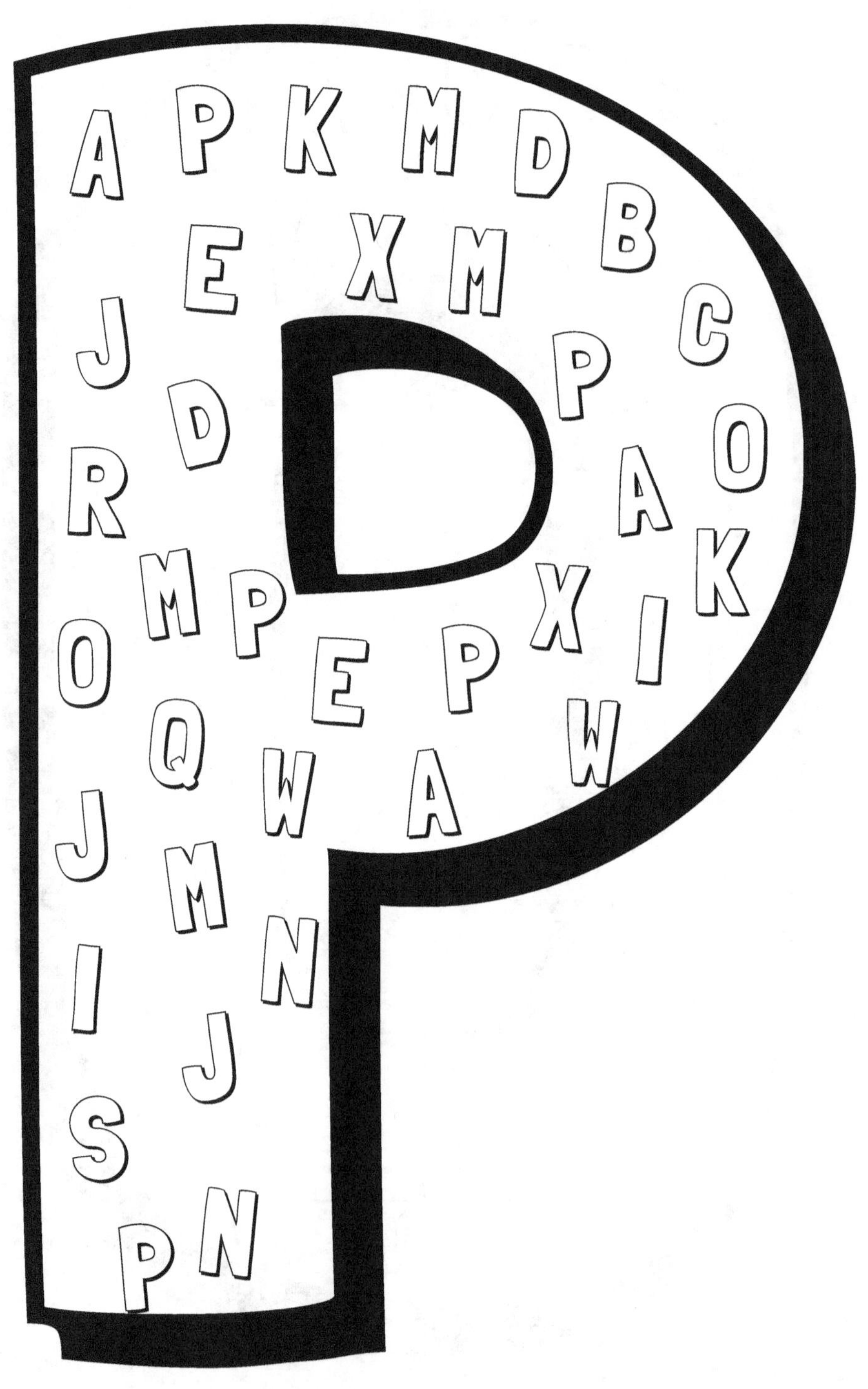

Letter Hunt

Find and color the letter Q

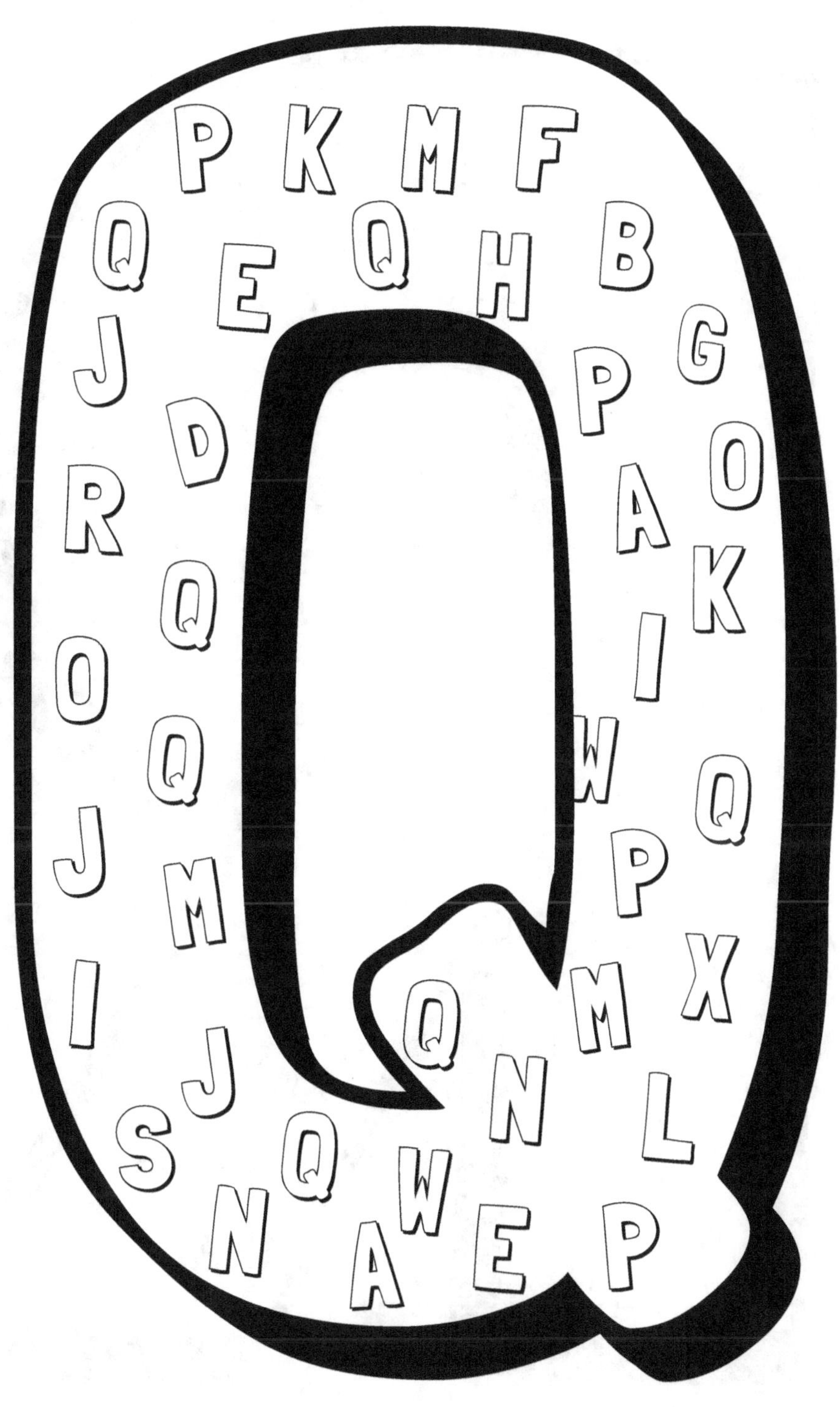

Letter Hunt

Find and color the letter R

Letter Hunt

Find and color the letter S

Letter Hunt

Find and color the letter T

Letter Hunt

Find and color the letter U

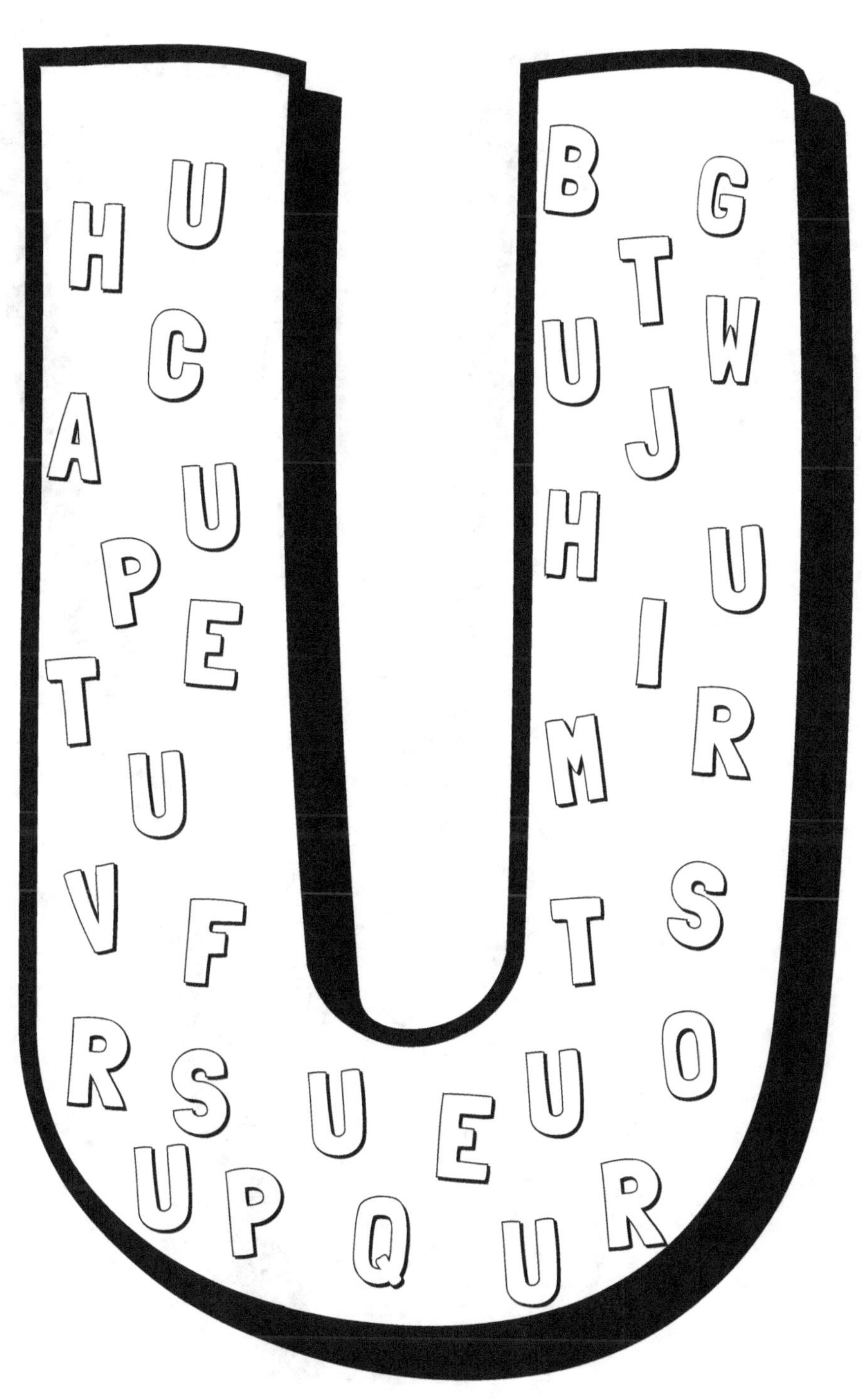

Letter Hunt

Find and color the letter V

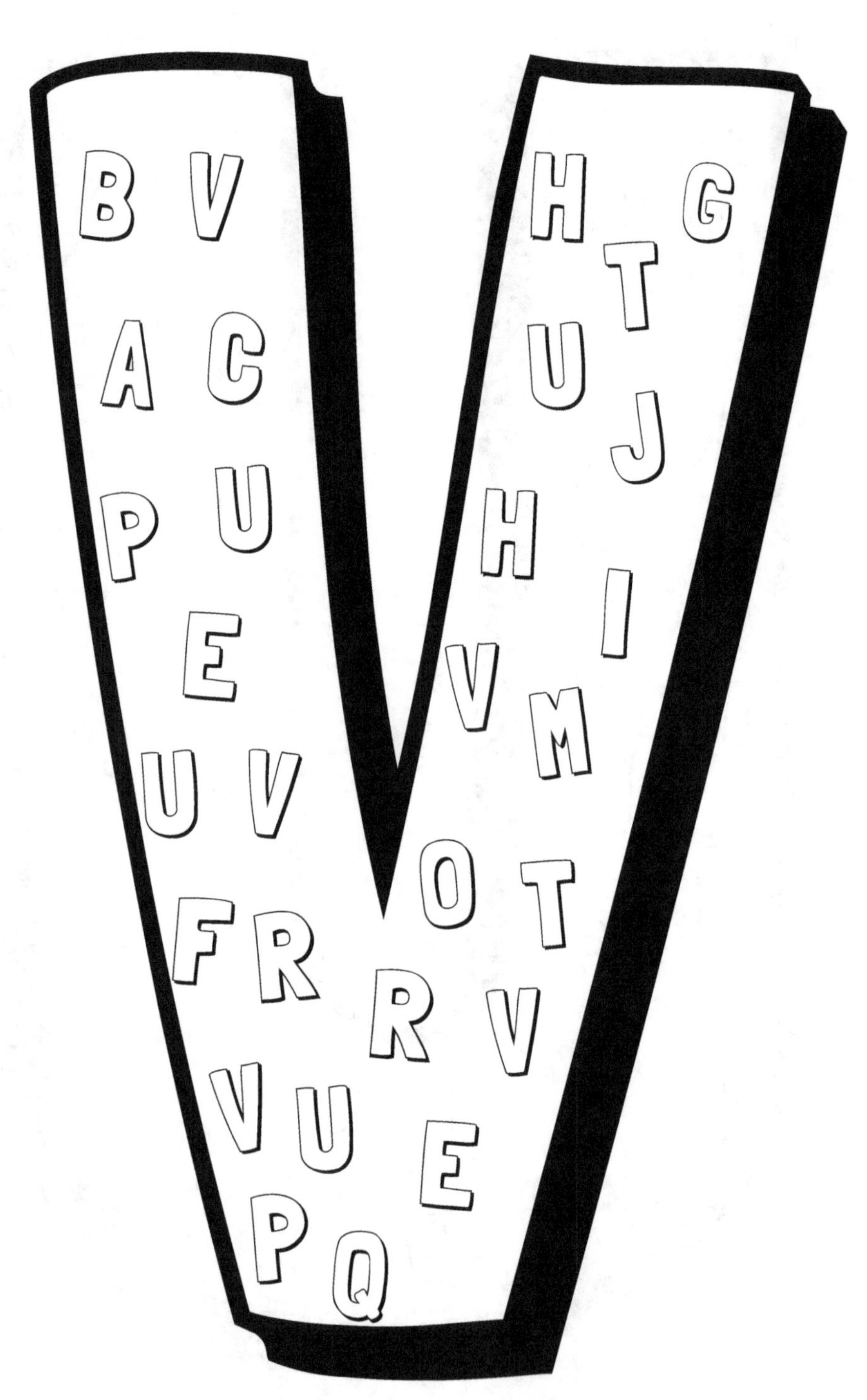

Letter Hunt

Find and color the letter W

Letter Hunt

Find and color the letter X

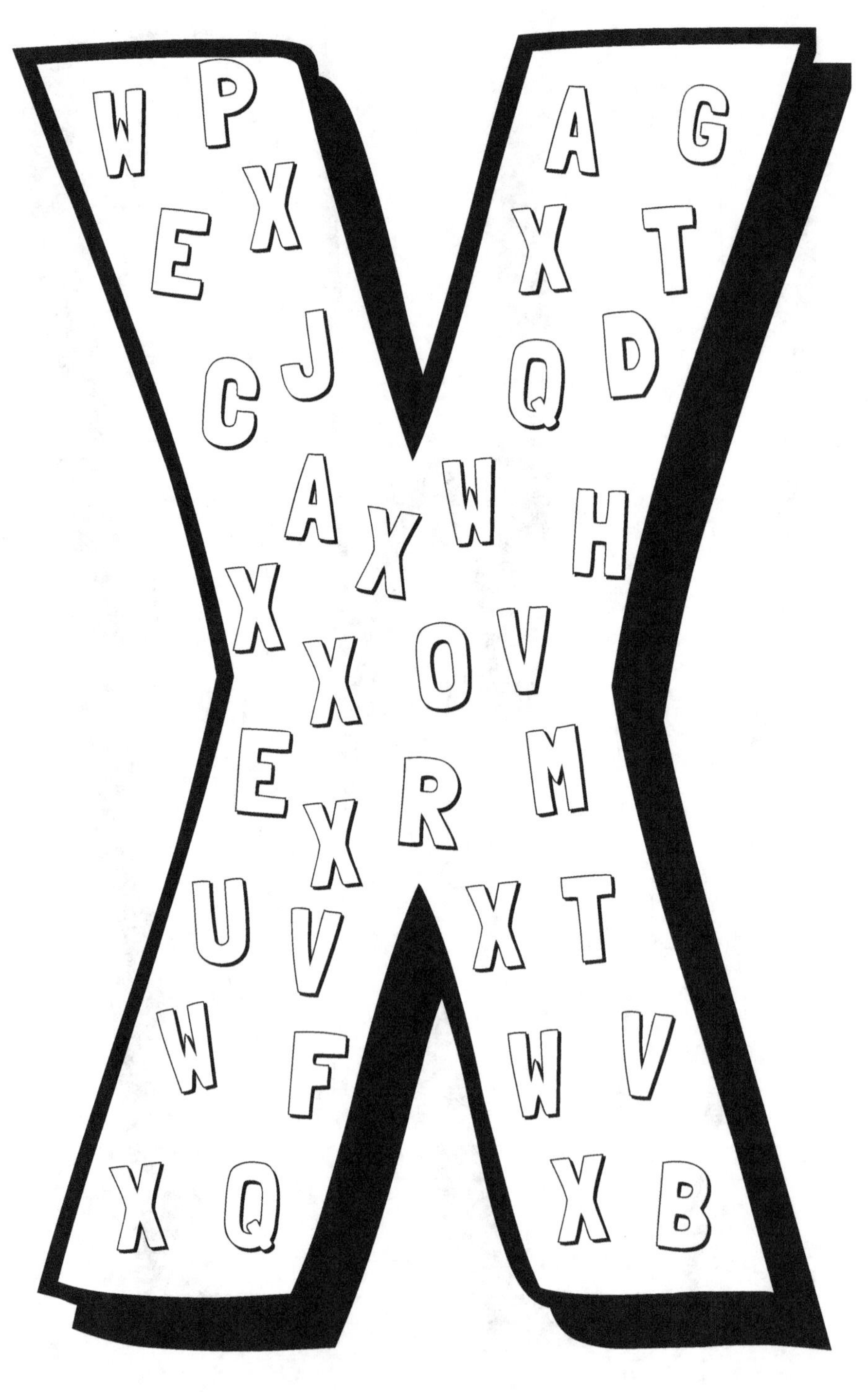

Letter Hunt

Find and color the letter Y

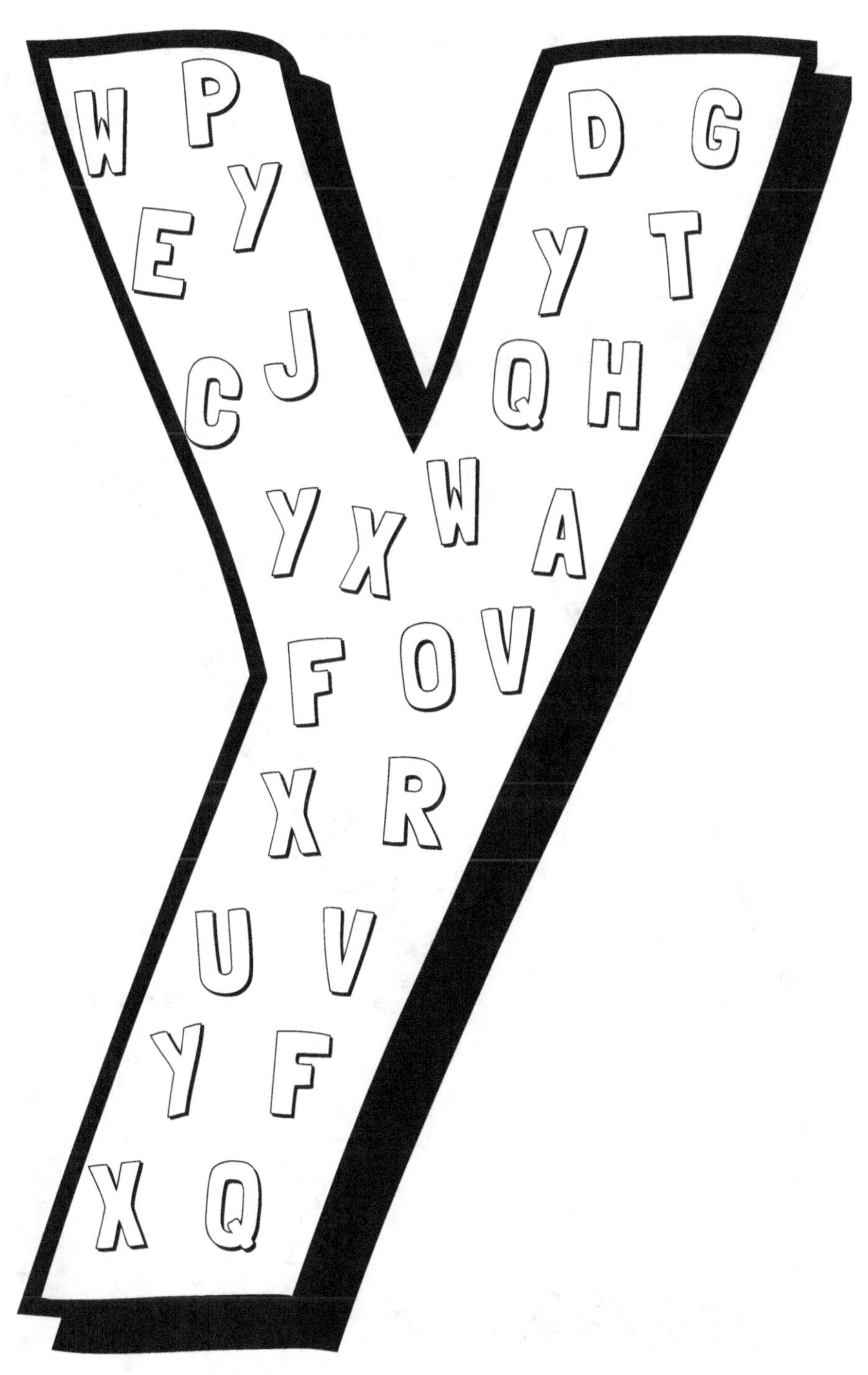

Letter Hunt

Find and color the letter Z

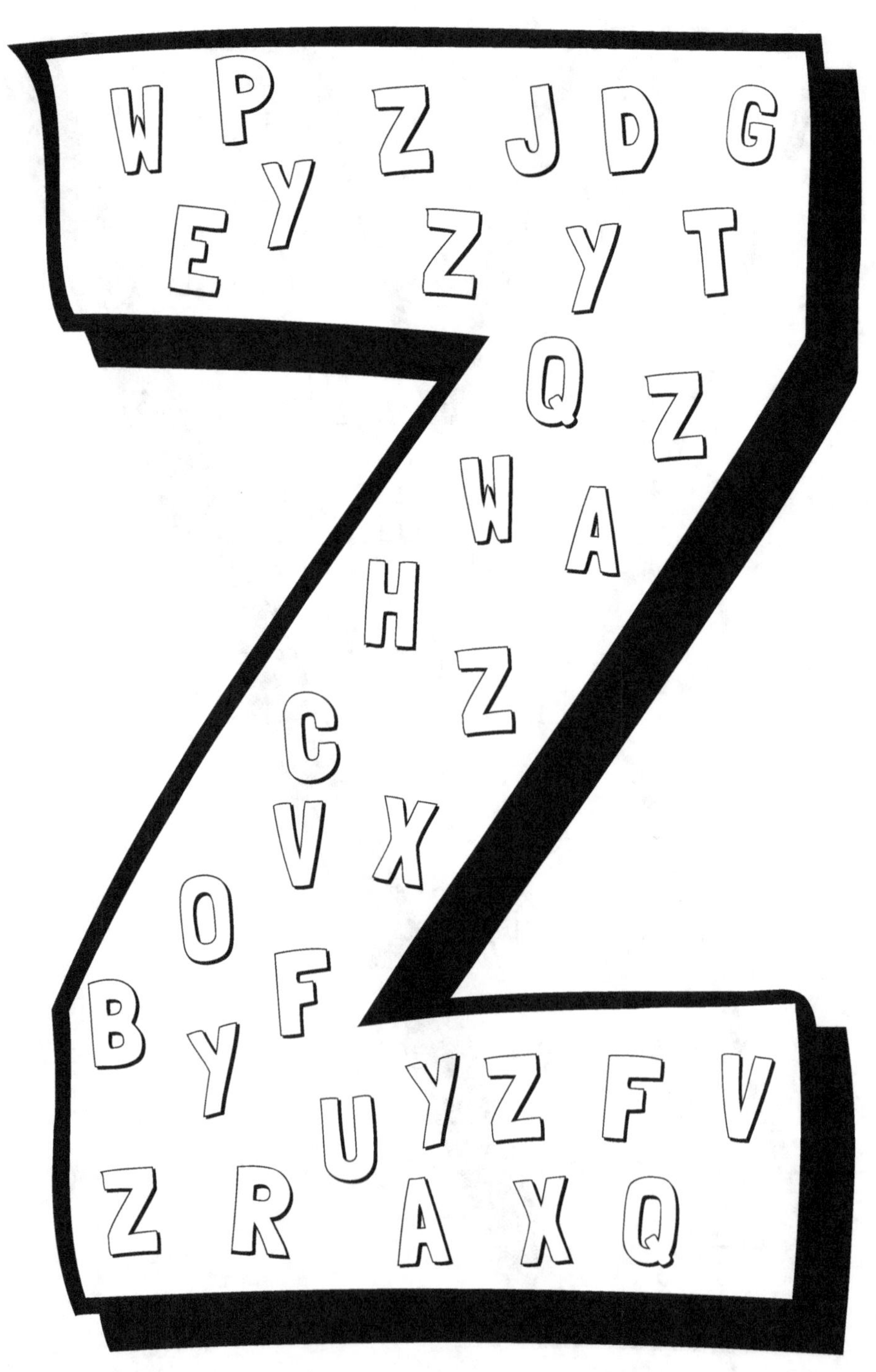

Beginning Letters

Say the name of the object and color the letter it begins with.

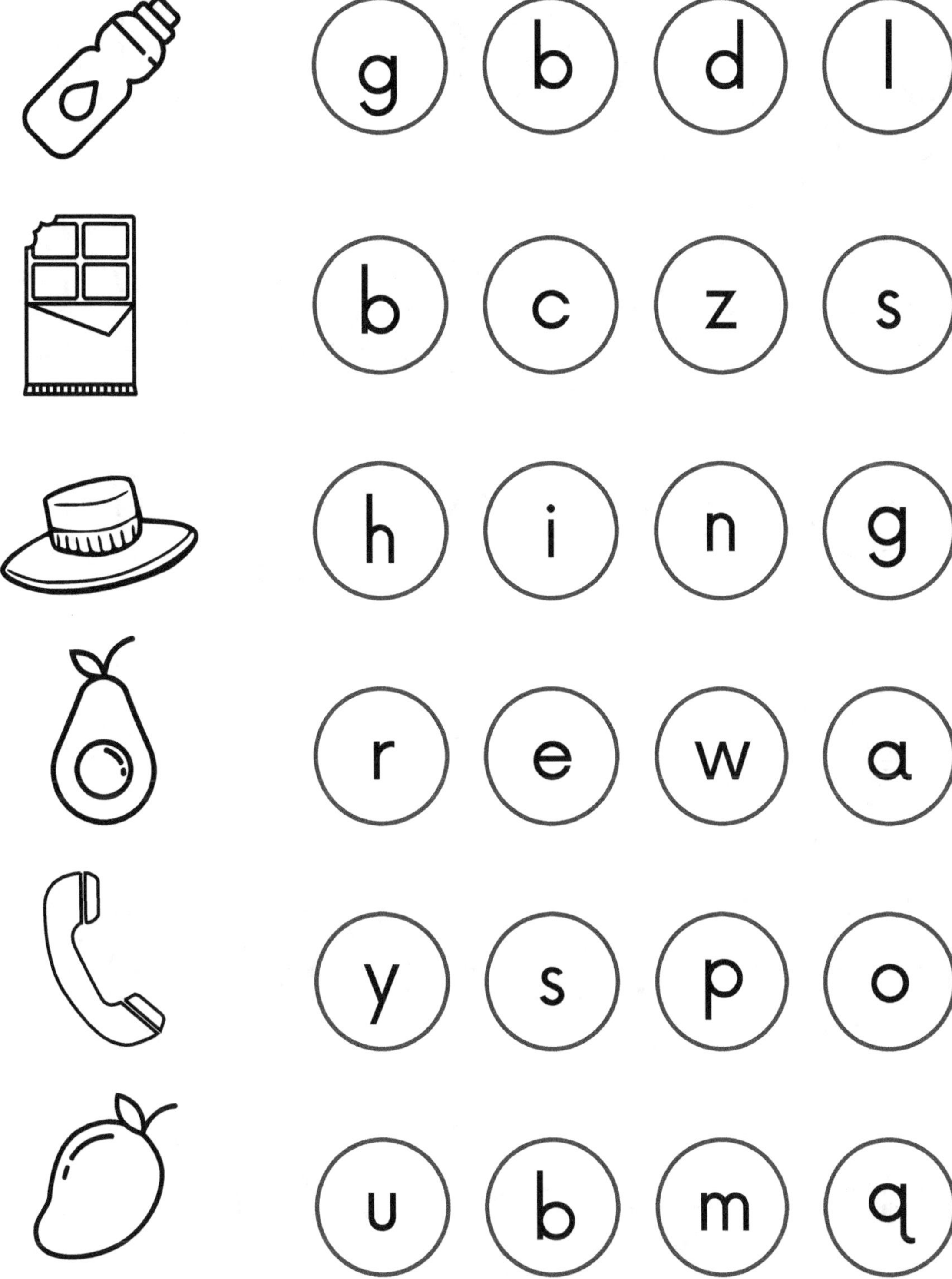

Beginning Letters

Say the name of the object and color the letter it begins with.

Beginning Letters

Say the name of the object and color the letter it begins with.

Beginning Letters

Say the name of the object and color the letter it begins with.

What letter is next?

D E F ◯   L M N ◯

S T U ◯   P Q R ◯

A B C ◯   H I J ◯

O P Q ◯   V W X ◯

What letter is next?

Q R S ◯   J K L ◯

C D E ◯   V Q U ◯

R S T ◯   M N O ◯

G H I ◯   U V W ◯

learn 10 colors

RED
RED

BLUE
BLUE

YELLOW
YELLOW

VIOLET
VIOLET

BLACK

ORANGE
ORANGE

PINK
PINK

BROWN
BROWN

GREEN
GREEN

WHITE
WHITE

mixing 10 colors

Color these things in the 3 primary colors.

RED RED **BLUE** BLUE **YELLOW** YELLOW

**Mixing them together creates new colors called secondary colors!
Try mixing them with paint and see what colors you get.**

 +  = 

RED RED **BLUE** BLUE **VIOLET** VIOLET

 +  = 

YELLOW YELLOW **RED** RED **ORANGE** ORANGE

 +  = 

BLUE BLUE **YELLOW** YELLOW **GREEN** GREEN

IDENTIFY THE OBJECT

Use the letters below to spell out the name of the object

Identify the Object

Use the letters below to spell out the name of the object

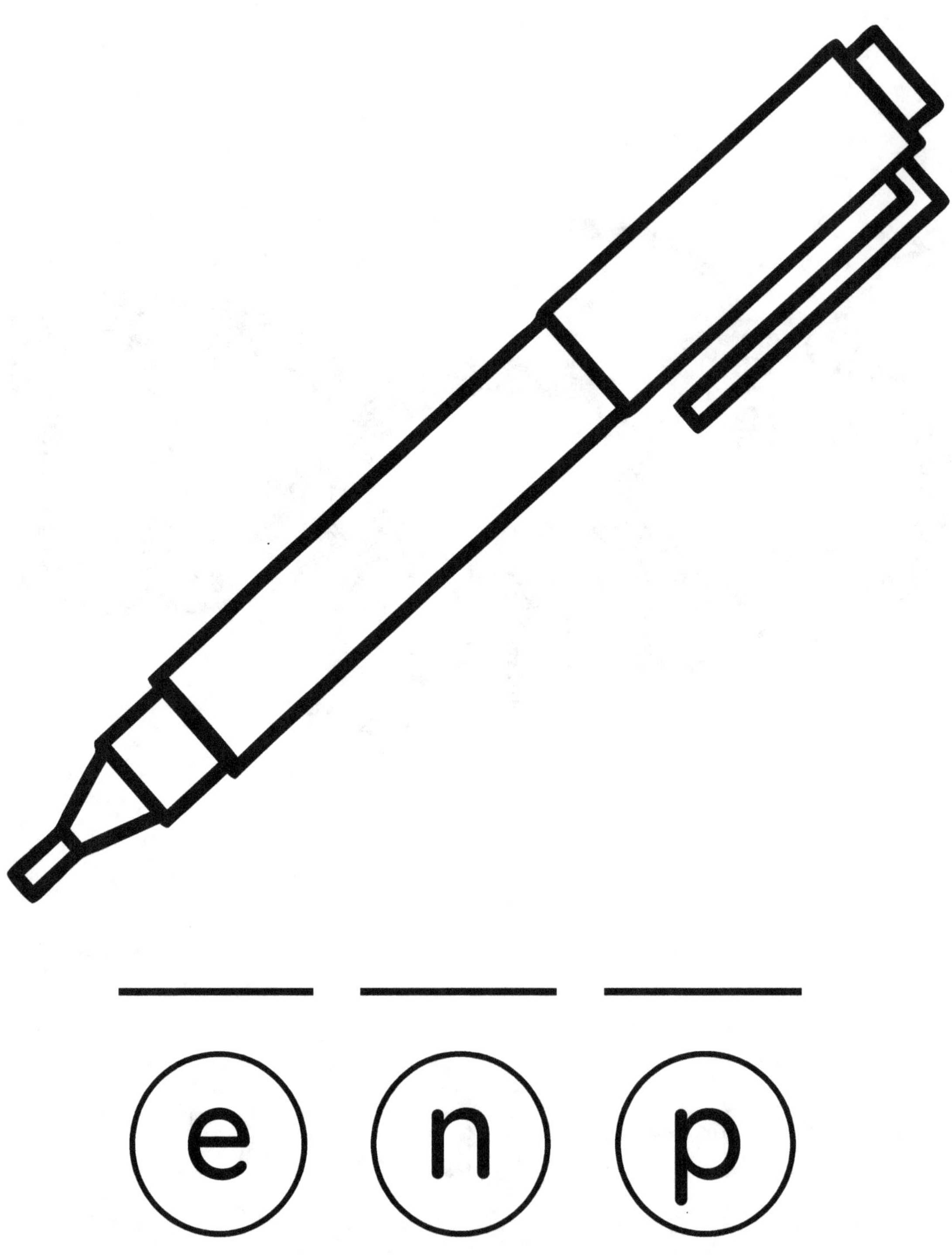

___ ___ ___

(e) (n) (p)

IDENTIFY THE OBJECT

Use the letters below to spell out the name of the object

___ ___ ___

Identify the Object

Use the letters below to spell out the name of the object

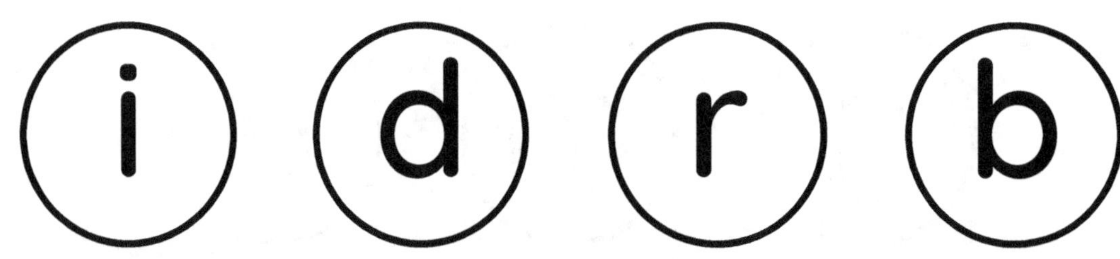

IDENTIFY THE OBJECT

Use the letters below to spell out the name of the object

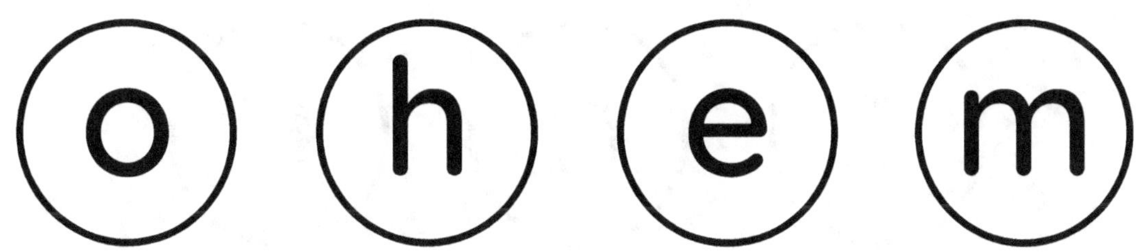

Identify the Object

Use the letters below to spell out the name of the object

Identify the Object

Use the letters below to spell out the name of the object

___ ___ ___

Identify the Object

Use the letters below to spell out the name of the object

Identify the Object

Use the letters below to spell out the name of the object

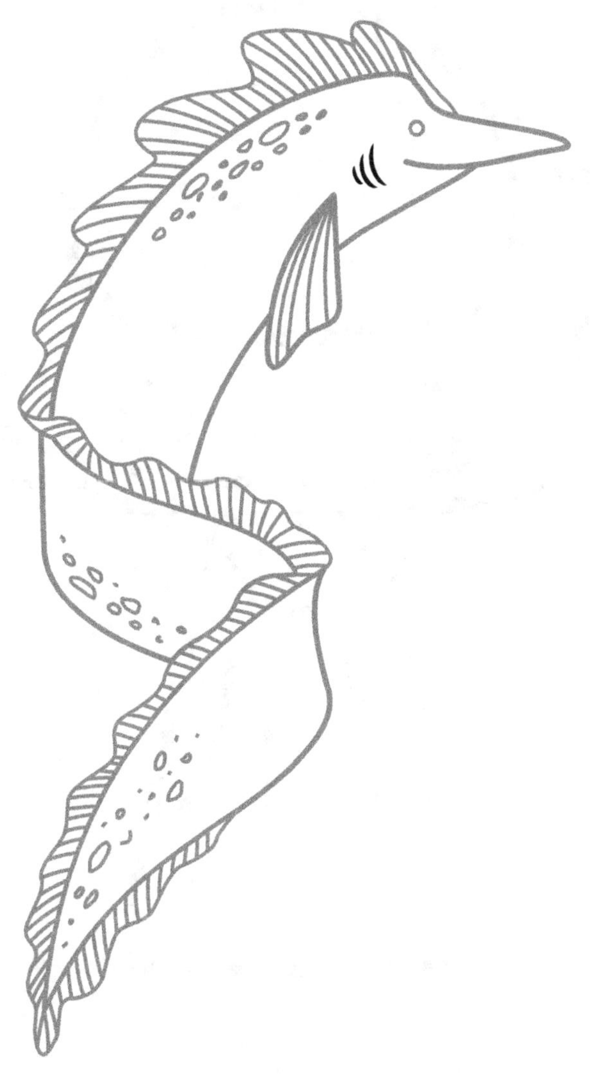

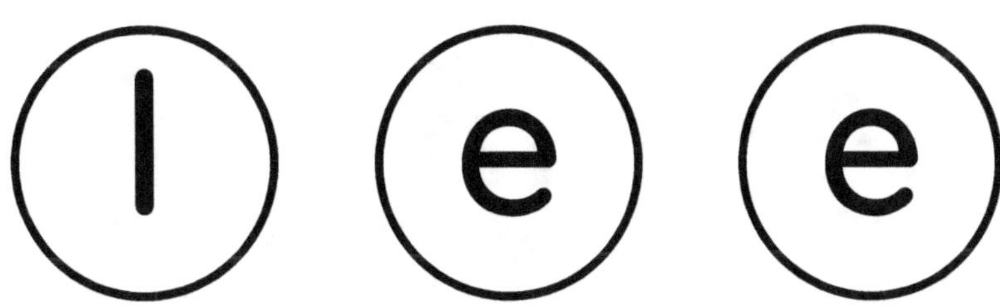

Identify the Object

Use the letters below to spell out the name of the object

IDENTIFY THE OBJECT

Use the letters below to spell out the name of the object

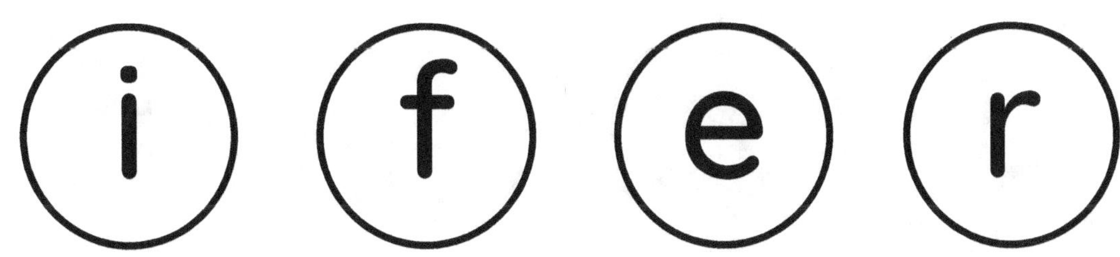

Identify the Object

Use the letters below to spell out the name of the object

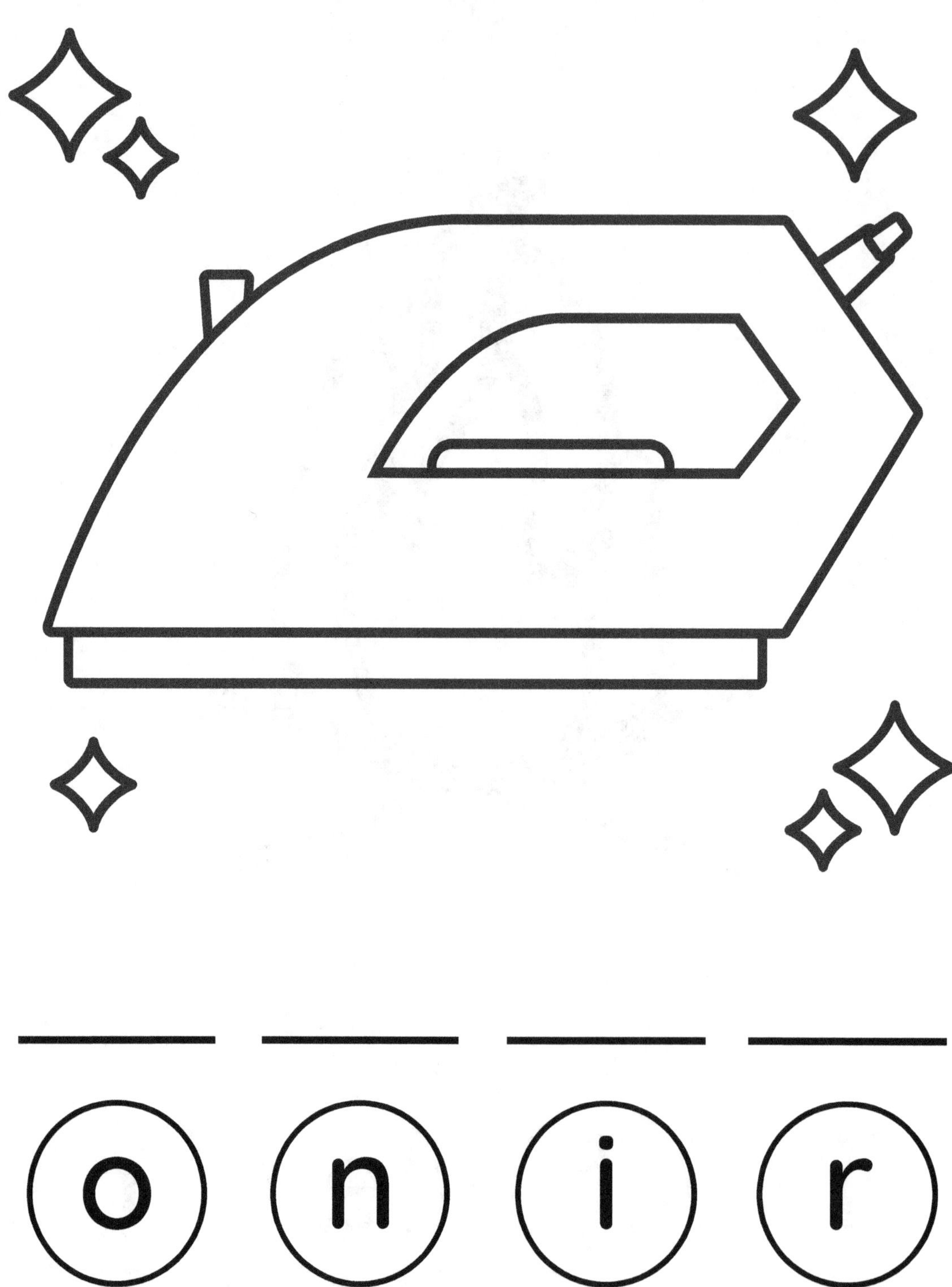

Identify the Object

Use the letters below to spell out the name of the object

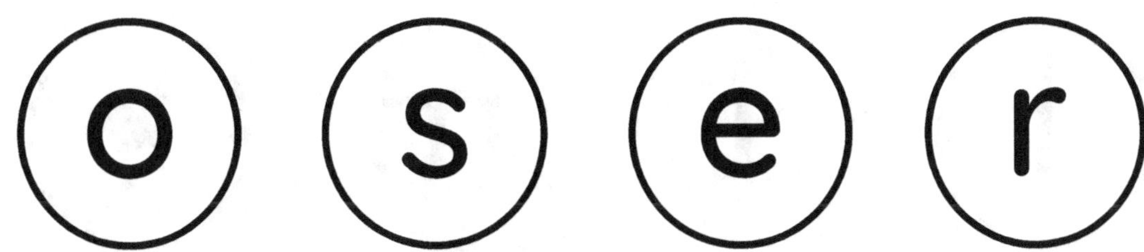

Identify the Object

Use the letters below to spell out the name of the object

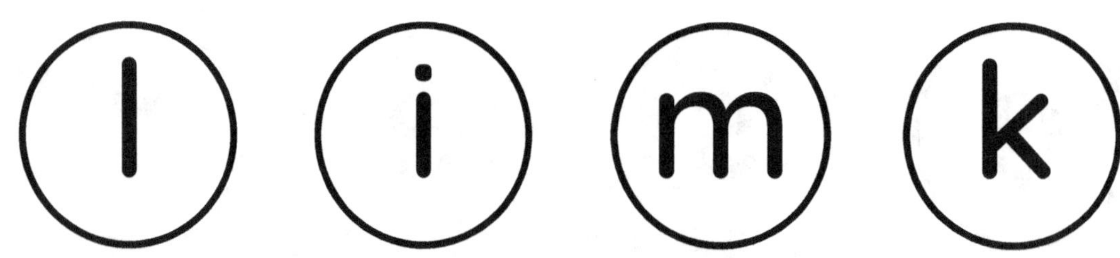

IDENTIFY THE OBJECT

Use the letters below to spell out the name of the object

IDENTIFY THE OBJECT

Use the letters below to spell out the name of the object

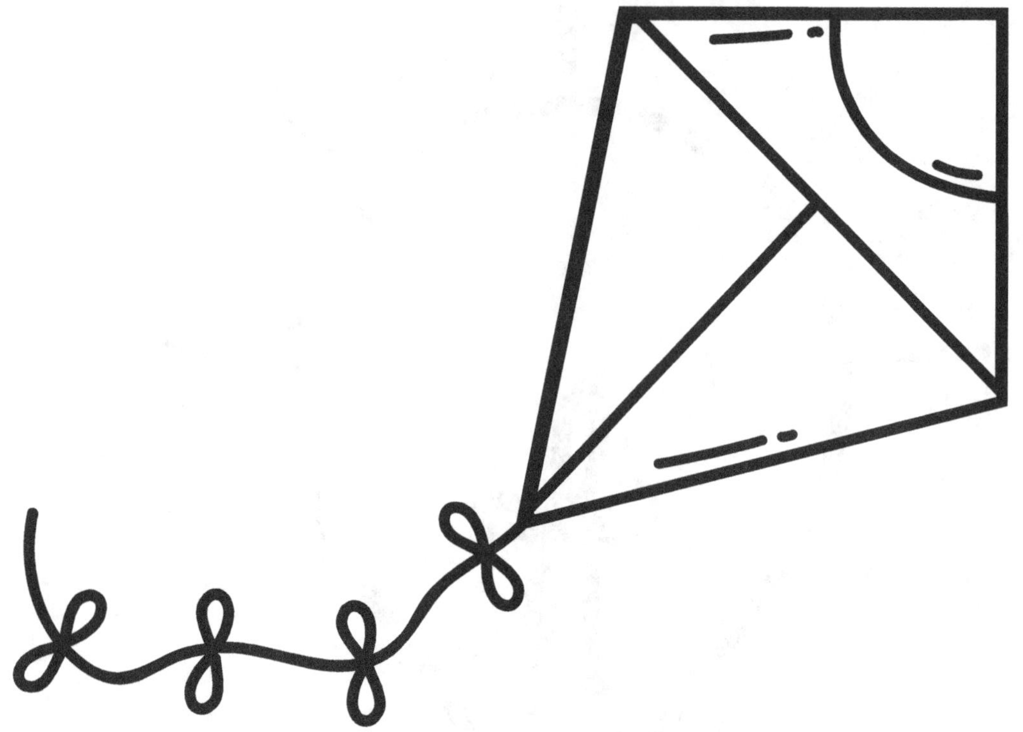

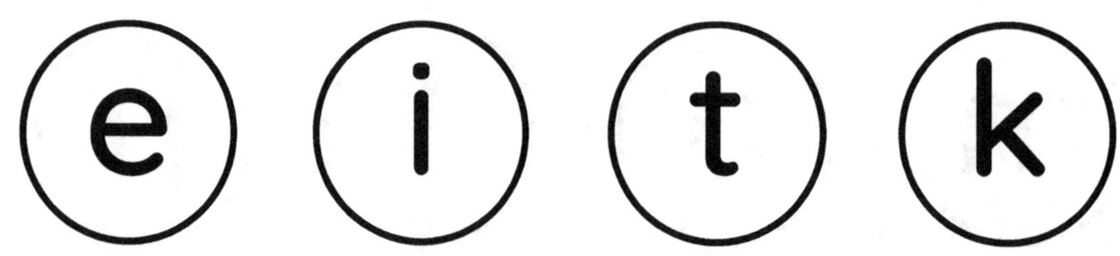

Identify the Object

Use the letters below to spell out the name of the object

____ ____ ____ ____

h s o e

IDENTIFY THE OBJECT

Use the letters below to spell out the name of the object

____ ____ ____ ____

s n t e

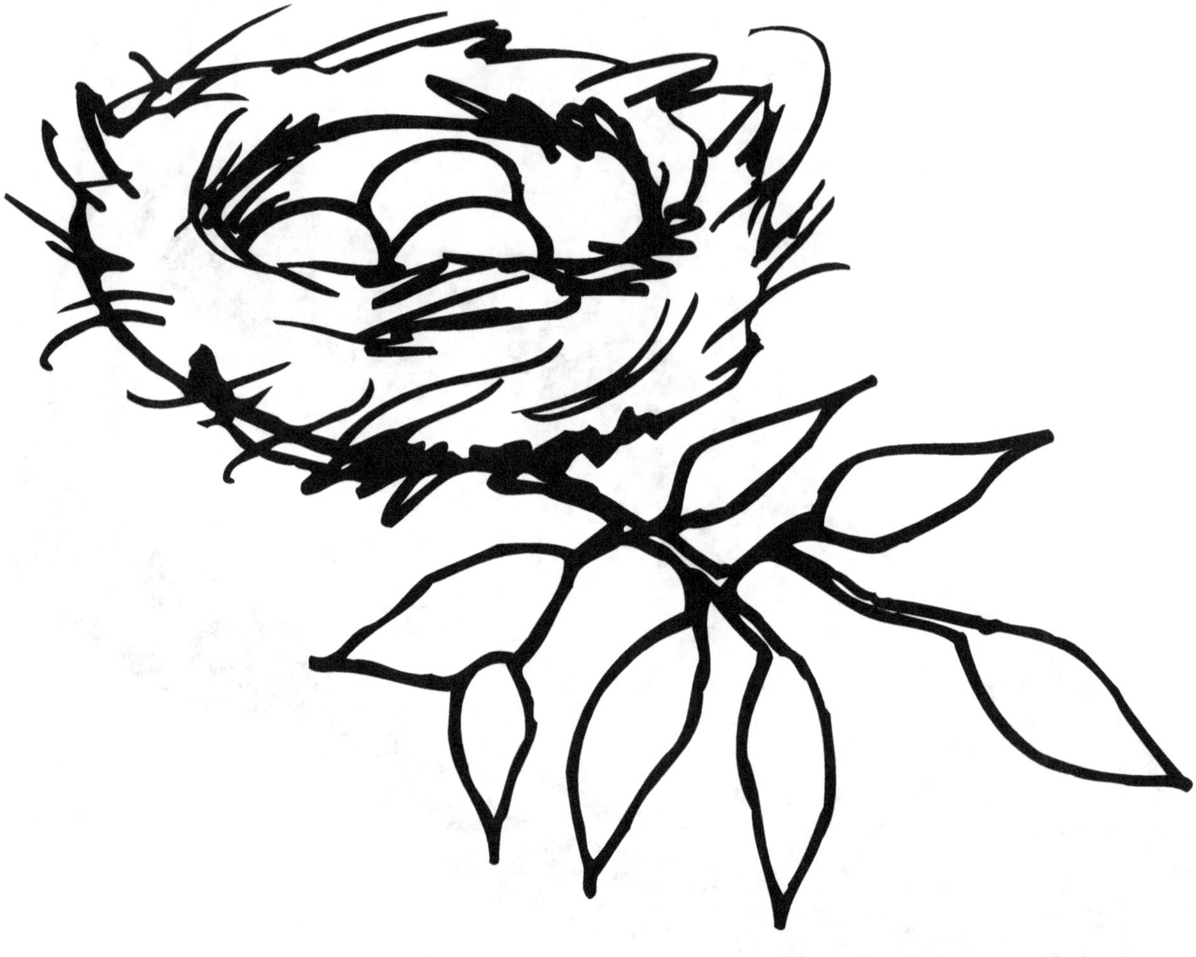

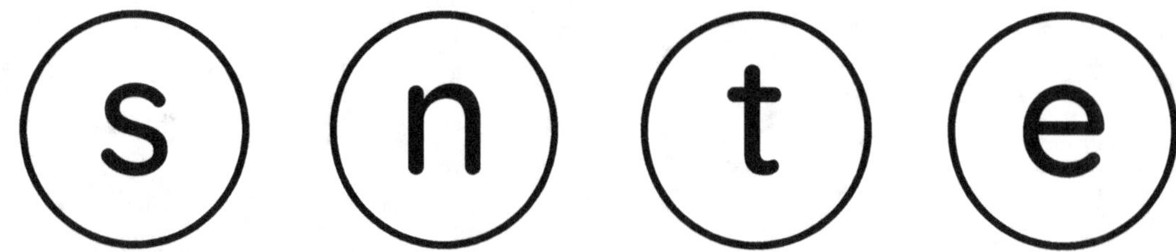

Identify the Object

Use the letters below to spell out the name of the object

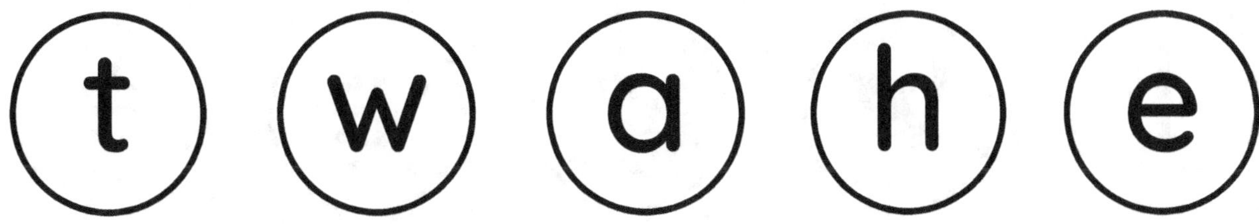

IDENTIFY THE OBJECT

Use the letters below to spell out the name of the object

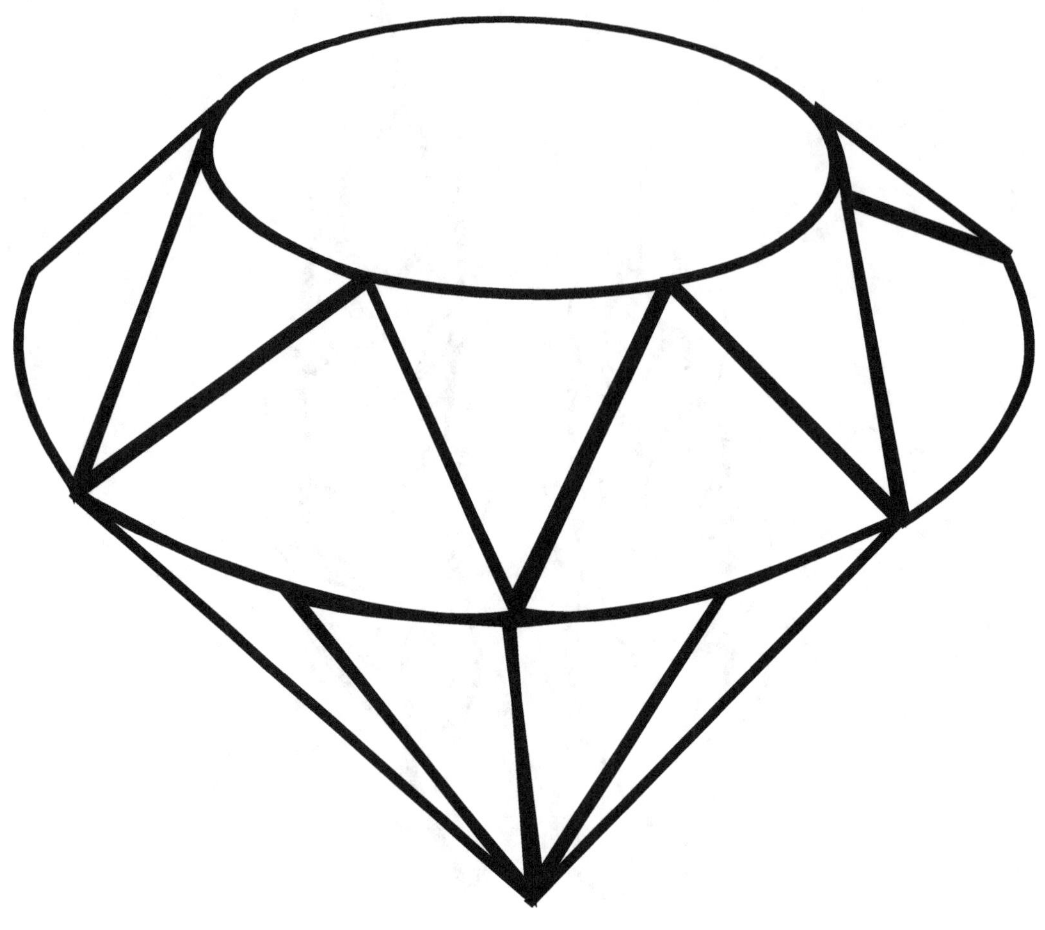

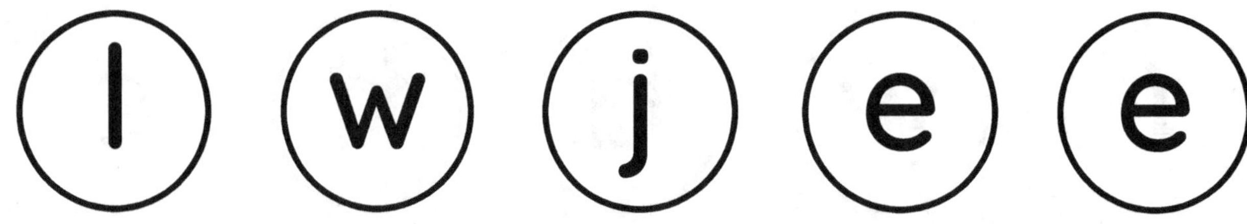

Identify the Object

Use the letters below to spell out the name of the object

___ ___ ___ ___ ___ ___

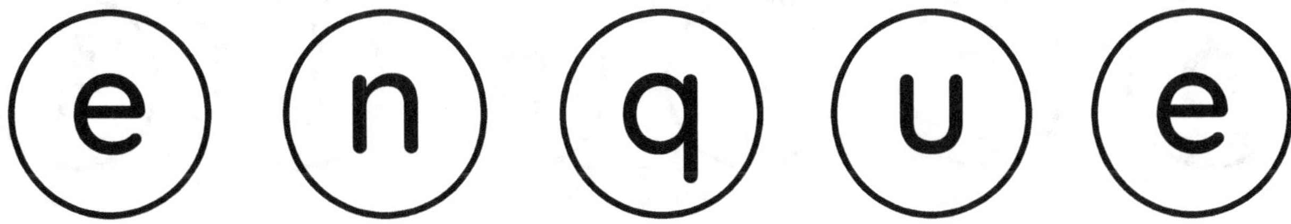

IDENTIFY THE OBJECT

Use the letters below to spell out the name of the object

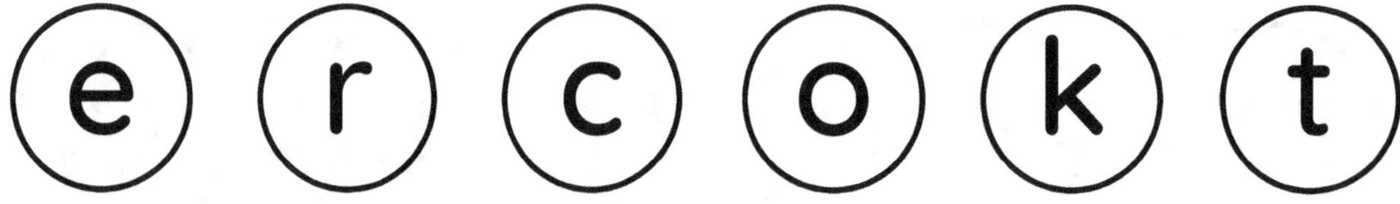

DAYS OF THE WEEK

Trace the letters to spell out the days.

MONTHS OF THE YEAR

Trace the letters to spell out the months.

Answer Key

Spot the Letters

Look at the letter on the left and circle the same letters on the row.

b	(b)	o	c	d	(b)	e
k	d	m	(k)	l	(k)	(k)
e	j	(e)	v	m	(e)	k
c	(c)	a	c	d	(c)	e
o	(o)	m	n	(o)	f	l
q	g	h	i	k	p	(q)
z	x	w	(z)	(z)	s	q

Spot the Letters

Look at the letter on the left and circle the same letters on the row.

d	b	o	c	(d)	b	e
p	d	m	k	l	(p)	(p)
j	(j)	w	v	m	e	(j)
t	w	a	(t)	d	c	(t)
n	i	m	(n)	o	(n)	l
g	(g)	h	i	(g)	p	q
i	j	w	m	l	k	(i)

Beginning Letters

Say the name of the object and color the letter it begins with.

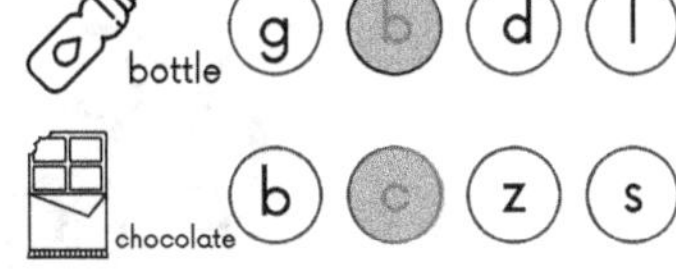
bottle — g **b** d l

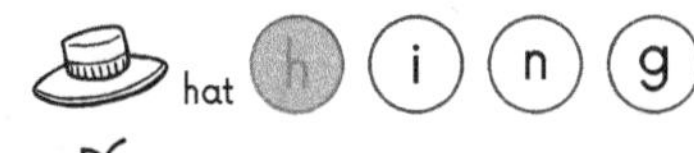
chocolate — b **c** z s

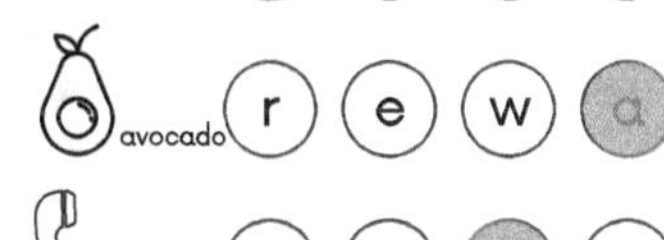
hat — **h** i n g

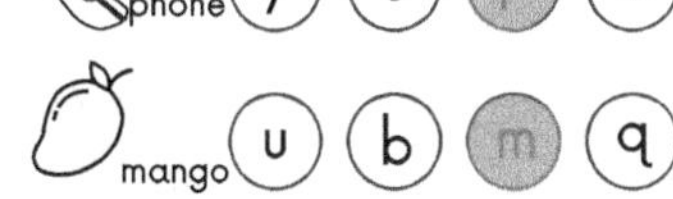
avocado — r e w **a**

phone — y s **p** o

mango — u b **m** q

Beginning Letters

Say the name of the object and color the letter it begins with.

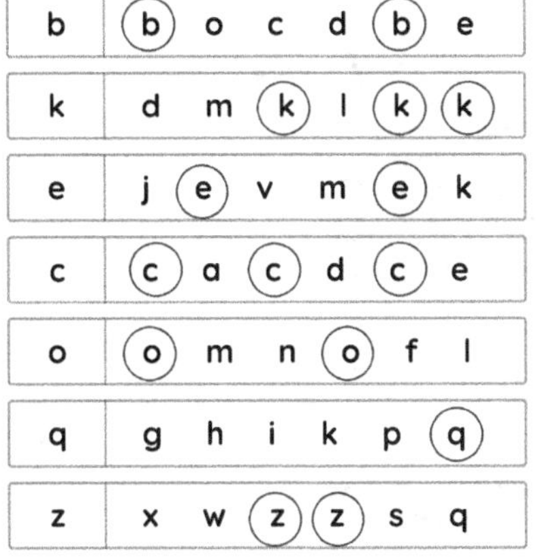

kangaroo — g f **k** l

van — a d k **v**

bananas — t **b** k u

castle — b p **c** f

bed — s t **b** d

owl — e **o** n y

Beginning Letters

Say the name of the object and color the letter it begins with.

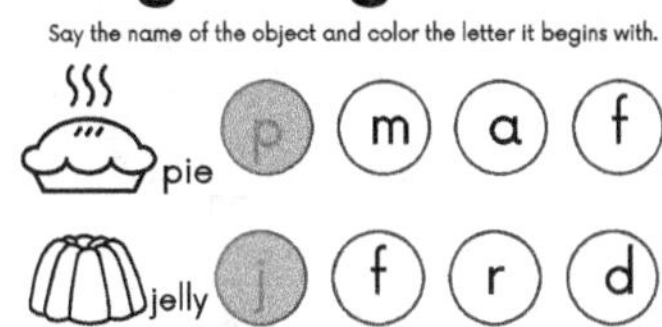
pie — **p** m a f

jelly — **j** f r d

shark — w n h **s**

ice cream — t y **i** o

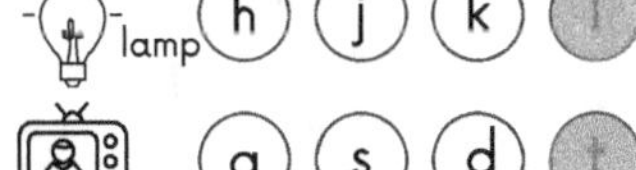
lamp — h j k **l**

television — a s d **t**

Beginning Letters

Say the name of the object and color the letter it begins with.

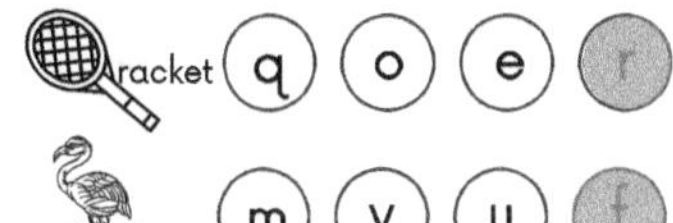
racket — q o e **r**

famingo — m y u **f**

sofa — **s** p l k

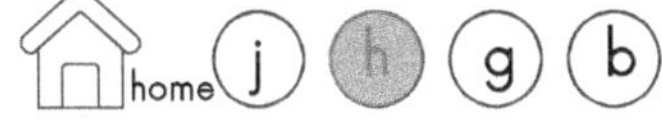
home — j **h** g b

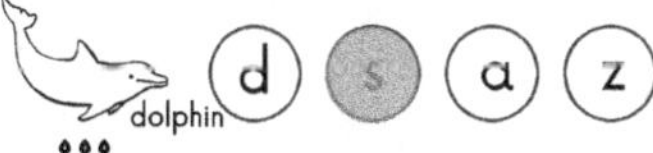
dolphin — d **s** a z

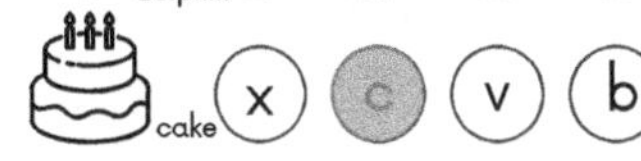
cake — x **c** v b

What letter is next?

Look at the following letters and write down what you think is next in the circle.

D E F (G)	L M N (O)
S T U (V)	P Q R (S)
A B C (D)	H I J (K)
O P Q (R)	V W X (Y)

What letter is next?

Look at the following letters and write down what you think is next in the circle.

Q R S (T)	J K L (M)
C D E (F)	U V W (X)
R S T (U)	M N O (P)
G H I (J)	T U V (W)

Answer Key

Identify the Object
Use the letters below to spell out the name of the object

a n t

(n) (t) (a)

Identify the Object
Use the letters below to spell out the name of the object

p e n

(e) (n) (p)

Identify the Object
Use the letters below to spell out the name of the object

m u g

(g) (m) (u)

Identify the Object
Use the letters below to spell out the name of the object

b i r d

(i) (d) (r) (b)

Identify the Object
Use the letters below to spell out the name of the object

h o m e

(o) (h) (e) (m)

Identify the Object
Use the letters below to spell out the name of the object

c a r

(r) (a) (c)

Identify the Object
Use the letters below to spell out the name of the object

d o g

(d) (g) (o)

Identify the Object
Use the letters below to spell out the name of the object

o w l

(w) (l) (o)

Identify the Object
Use the letters below to spell out the name of the object

e e l

(l) (e) (e)

Answer Key

Identify the Object
Use the letters below to spell out the name of the object

u f o

o u f

Identify the Object
Use the letters below to spell out the name of the object

f i r e

i f e r

Identify the Object
Use the letters below to spell out the name of the object

i r o n

o n i r

Identify the Object
Use the letters below to spell out the name of the object

r o s e

o s e r

Identify the Object
Use the letters below to spell out the name of the object

m i l k

l i m k

Identify the Object
Use the letters below to spell out the name of the object

l a m p

m a l p

Identify the Object
Use the letters below to spell out the name of the object

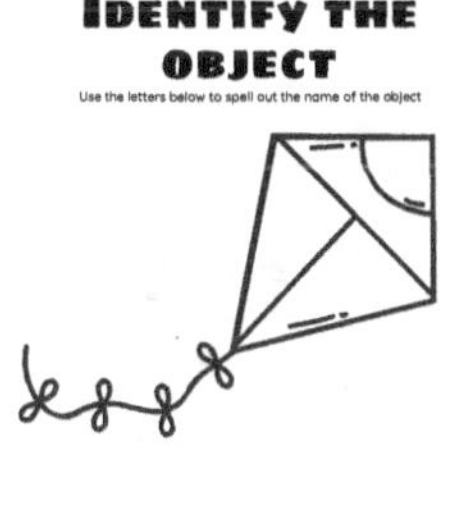

k i t e

e i t k

Identify the Object
Use the letters below to spell out the name of the object

s h o e

h s o e

Identify the Object
Use the letters below to spell out the name of the object

n e s t

s n t e

Answer Key

Identify the Object

Use the letters below to spell out the name of the object

w h e a t

(t) (w) (a) (h) (e)

Identify the Object

Use the letters below to spell out the name of the object

j e w e l

(l) (w) (j) (e) (e)

Identify the Object

Use the letters below to spell out the name of the object

q u e e n

(e) (n) (q) (u) (e)

Identify the Object

Use the letters below to spell out the name of the object

r o c k e t

(e) (r) (c) (o) (k) (t)

www.ingramcontent.com/pod-product-compliance
Lightning Source LLC
Chambersburg PA
CBHW081403130726
47998CB00011B/3059